A Decade of Ghana

A Decade of Ghana

Politics, Economy and Society

2004–2013

By

Michael Amoah
Kwesi Aning
Nancy Annan
Paul Nugent

BRILL
LEIDEN | BOSTON

This publication has been typeset in the multilingual 'Brill' typeface. With over 5,100 characters covering Latin, IPA, Greek, and Cyrillic, this typeface is especially suitable for use in the humanities.
For more information, please see www.brill.com/brill-typeface.

ISBN 978-90-04-30818-3

This book is printed on acid-free paper.

Contents

Ghana in 2004

Paul Nugent

The year was thoroughly dominated by the run-up to the presidential and parliamentary elections that were held on 7 December. Apart from the preparatory work carried out by the National Electoral Commission (NEC), most aspects of everyday policy and governance, including the budget, were interpreted in the light of the forthcoming polls. The proceedings of the National Reconciliation Commission (NRC) and the continuing fall-out from the murder of the Ya Na (king of Dagomba) and up to 40 of his retainers in 2002, were similarly highly charged. Even President Kufuor's attempts to mediate in the Ivorian crisis served as a heated debating point between the government and the National Democratic Congress (NDC). The electoral contest itself, which brought victory for the incumbent New Patriotic Party (NPP), was far more evenly matched than most observers expected, and confirmed the entrenchment of a two-party system.

Domestic Politics

At the start of 2004, the efforts on the part of NEC to resolve a number of looming problems in the election process proved contentious. One problem, which had become apparent during the 2000 polls, was that there was a large disparity in the size of constituencies. Moreover, the uneven rate of population increase threatened to create further distortions. The chairman of NEC, Dr. Kwadwo Afari-Djan, justified the creation of *30 new constituencies* on the basis that they were the most appropriate way of resolving

 | DOI 10.1163/9789004308183_002

the anomalies. Although the opposition parties were suspicious – especially when NPP General Secretary Dan Botwe tactlessly stated that NPP should by rights win all the new constituencies that it had helped to create – the process did eventually win broad acceptance. In fact, far greater disagreement was caused by the creation of 28 new districts (whose boundaries cannot cross-cut constituencies) by virtue of the competition over the choice of new district capitals. In some cases, such as Adaklu-Anyigbe district (Volta region), this had a dramatic effect on the parliamentary campaign when what should have been an extremely safe NDC seat almost fell to an independent candidate. Another bone of contention was the *electoral register*, which most people agreed was grossly inflated in 2000. The NEC presided over the compilation of a new register and the issuing of photographic identification cards. The latter proved logistically difficult and many concerns were expressed about the likely disenfranchisement of large numbers of voters. However, the NEC, which remained in close contact with all the political parties, was able to resolve the problems to the satisfaction of most.

Kufuor and the NPP campaigned for re-election on the basis that the government had managed the economy successfully and had demonstrated its sincere commitment to 'zero tolerance' on corruption. On 8 September, Kufuor launched the NPP manifesto with a pledge to create an office of accountability within the presidency, if he was re-elected. The NPP also reminded Ghanaians of the poor standards of public accountability that had prevailed under the last NDC regime, as a result of which a number of ministers were incarcerated. The NPP also claimed that John Atta-Mills of NDC would not be his own man, but would be beholden to former President *Flight-Lieutenant Jerry Rawlings*, who played the key role in securing his renomination ahead of Dr. Kwesi Botchway (a respected former finance minister from the 1980s). The fact that Rawlings was so prominent on the campaign trail made this claim seem more credible. A recurrent theme in his rabble-rousing speeches was that Kufuor planned to rig the elections. In the run-up to the polls, the government claimed to have uncovered a coup plot, involving members of '64 Battallion'. Rawlings had created the latter as a counterweight to the army during the 1980s, but it had been disbanded during the return to democracy, while its commanding officer, Lt.-Colonel Larry Gbevlo-Lartey, had retrained as a lawyer. The authorities produced no credible evidence of a conspiracy and much of the independent press interpreted the announcement as a scare tactic. It also came against the backdrop of the NRC *hearings* in which Ghanaians were reminded of human rights abuses that had taken place under previous Rawlings administrations. The NRC, which borrowed from the model of the South African Truth and Reconciliation Commission, was extremely contentious from the start, with the NDC claiming that there was no need for such a body and that the NPP was seeking to carry out a witch-hunt. The allegation that *Kojo Tsikata* (a leading member of the former Provisional National Defence Council in the 1980s), and possibly Rawlings himself, had been complicit in the murder of three judges and a retired army officer in 1982 resurfaced at the hearings. The appearance of the two men before the NRC was itself seen as a victory of sorts by government sympathisers, although disappointment was expressed at how little was actually revealed. Though the NRC report had not appeared by the end of the year, sections were leaked to the press in the period before the elections in what appeared to be a blatant attempt to influence voter perceptions.

The NDC, on the other hand, insisted that Kufuor's economic programme hurt the poorest sections of society. The leadership disputed Kufuor's claim to have clean hands and pointed to a number of mini-scandals as merely the tip of the *corruption* iceberg. This included 'Bambagate', named after Alhaji Moctar

Bamba, a deputy minister and deputy chief of staff in the office of the president, who was exposed for using official letterheads to secure loans for private companies he was involved in. When Bamba resigned, the information minister (Nana Akomea) hastily reassured Ghanaians that this did not preclude a criminal investigation. However, NDC claimed that corruption went much deeper and there was bound to be an official cover-up. The NDC could also refer to Ghana's 'Transparency International' ratings, which slipped from 51 to 73 out of 133 countries. However, NDC failed to come up with a big enough scoop to seriously tarnish the image of the Kufuor administration, even if some of the independent press (notably the 'Ghanaian Chronicle') began to make potentially serious allegations.

The NDC had more success with the government's mishandling of the *crisis in Dagbon*, with its press accusing the administration of being either complicit in the killing of the Ya Na or failing to protect him. The struggle over Dagomba kingship has been a recurrent theme since independence, with successive governments siding with either the Abudu or the Andani clan in a complex system of alliances. In 1987, the supreme court had confirmed the principle of rotation as well as the incumbency of Yakubu Andani II, something the Abudu militants never accepted. In March 2002, the government was aware of escalating tensions between the two factions. When violence threatened to break out in Yendi, a curfew was imposed but was subsequently rescinded. Thereafter, the palace was attacked, the Ya Na was beheaded and possibly as many as 40 members of his retinue were brutally killed. The government stood accused of failing to protect the Dagomba king because the police and soldiers posted to the crisis area unaccountably failed to intervene. All the most prominent Dagombas associated with the regime originated on the Abudu side, which is not surprising in view of their historic alignment with the Busia/Danquah tradition (Ghanaian leaders from the

1960s with which the NPP is associated). The list included *Vice-President Aliu Mahama*; the then minister of the interior and MP for Yendi, Alhaji Yakubu; Northern Regional Minister Imoro Andani; the national security advisor, General Joshua Hamidu; and the national security coordinator, Major Abukari Sulemana. This profile provided grounds for suspicion in itself, as did the revelation that the legal chambers of the then *attorney-general, Nana Akuffo-Addo*, had previously represented the Abudu faction. But even if there was no grand conspiracy, NDC partisans could argue that the government had adopted a very cavalier stance towards the safety of the Dagomba king, which would have been inconceivable if it had been the Asantehene (king of Ashanti) or the Okyenhene of Akyem whose life was in danger. The NDC expected to profit from a backlash in the northern region, and partly for this reason Atta-Mills chose a Dagomba MP, Muhammed Mumuni, as his running mate. The NDC press also exploited the concerns of non-Ashantis that the *Asantehene, Osei Tutu II*, was seeking to set himself up as the effective king of Ghana. Indeed, one newspaper claimed that Kufuor planned to change the constitution in order to turn the Asantehene into a constitutional monarch. This came on top of news of a substantial, and unprecedented, World Bank grant to the Asantehene to enable him to embark on a number of development initiatives.

Of the *smaller opposition parties*, most merely fielded a few parliamentary candidates. The exceptions were the Convention People's Party (CPP) and the People's National Convention (PNC), both of which claimed to be upholding the socialist ideals of Kwame Nkrumah, Ghana's first president. The CPP's former leader, George Hagan, bizarrely advised party supporters to vote for Kufuor rather than George Aggudey, who had succeeded him as the flag-bearer. Edward Mahama stood for president again, but on this occasion tried to forge a grand coalition between his PNC and Dan Lartey's Great Consolidated Popular Party (GCPP) and the Egle Party. When Mahama preferred Danny Ofori-Atta of the Egle Party as his running mate, Lartey walked out. The CPP and PNC both attacked NPP policies as being anti-poor, but they lacked the resources to carry their message to the Ghanaian people. Crucially, none of the newspapers championed their respective causes.

Although there was some violence around election time, most notably around Tamale (capital of the northern region) and around Kwamikrom (Volta region), the elections went ahead to the satisfaction of *independent observers* and most political parties, with the partial exception of NDC. Although the NPP won comfortably, it failed to achieve the total domination that it had confidently predicted. *Kufuor only narrowly avoided a run-off,* having secured just less than 52% of the vote to Atta-Mills's 45%. This was not a brilliant result for Kufuor, who had won 57% to Atta-Mills's 43% in the run-off four years earlier. In fact, Kufuor performed less well than his party did in the parliamentary elections (56% of seats). This was in spite of the fact that a number of rebels stood against official NPP candidates. Interestingly, while NPP made inroads into the regions that NDC had previously dominated (especially in the north, but also in Volta region), NDC reversed the pattern in some of the regions of NPP strength, including Ashanti. NPP received a particular shock in the *Greater Accra region,* where five new seats were created but the party ended up being one seat down. Remarkably, NDC gained six seats in the region. This highlighted the political volatility of the urban electorate, which began to complain of unfulfilled promises. Overall though, NPP gained a safe majority in parliament with 128 seats to 94 for NDC, four for PNC, three for CPP and a single independent. However, these results also underlined the fallacy of claims that had surrounded the hearings of the NRC to the effect that Ghanaians associated NDC with a reign of terror carried out under Rawlings. It would be fair to conclude that memories were divided over what had transpired over the previous two decades. The Northern region remained the weak link in Ghanaian democracy and the authorities had good cause to worry about the ferrying of weapons from Côte d'Ivoire into Dagbon. The death of the CPP regional chairman while in military custody, in the immediate aftermath of the elections, merely compounded an already tense situation. The government promised a full enquiry into the circumstances of Alhaji Mobila's death, but the credibility of the Kufuor government in the north was at a low ebb.

Foreign Affairs

Foreign policy has never been President Kufuor's strong suit, and it was widely observed that he has been more or less anonymous on the continental stage since 2000. However, the president had a highly articulate minister in the shape of *Nana Akuffo-Addo*, who had been moved to the foreign affairs portfolio after the Dagbon imbroglio. It was hoped that Kufuor might make his mark on the continental stage when he assumed office as *ECOWAS* chairman in 2004. With fellow Ghanaians *Kofi Annan and Ibn Chambas* holding the key positions of UN Secretary-General and executive secretary of ECOWAS respectively, the stage could hardly have been more favourably set. While Kufuor's profile certainly increased, the results were mixed. The single most pressing challenge facing him was the ongoing crisis in Côte d'Ivoire in which he attempted to mediate on several occasions. In March, opposition parties in the south declared their intention to defy a government ban and to demonstrate in Abidjan against President Laurent Gbagbo, whom they accused of seeking to wreck the Linas-Marcoussis peace accord. Kufuor sought to use his good offices to deflect a stand-off. However, he was ultimately unsuccessful in preventing a government crackdown on 25 March, which left up to 120 opposition supporters dead. At the end of July, all the protagonists in the wider crisis were invited to Accra to participate in a fresh round of peace talks, which were also attended by Kofi Annan, Thabo Mbeki, Olusegun Obasanjo and nine other African heads of state. With considerable pressure being applied to all sides in the conflict, a fresh timetable for *implementation of the Linas-Marcoussis accord was announced* on 30 July. The signatories agreed that the political reforms would be implemented by the end of August and that the disarmament programme would commence on 15 October. While this was a successful conclusion, there were fresh outbreaks of fighting in November when Gbagbo chose to bomb cities in the rebel-held north. The lack of tangible results led opposition politicians in Ghana to claim that Kufuor did not enjoy the confidence of the parties to the Ivorian dispute. Indeed, Alban Bagbin, the minority leader in parliament, went on the radio to announce that both the Burkinabe and Ivorian presidents had confided their lack of confidence in Kufuor. Both later categorically denied that this was the case in official communiqués, which the pro-NPP press subsequently sought to use to cause the maximum embarrassment to Bagbin.

On Ghana's eastern border, relationships with the Eyadéma regime remained as harmonious as ever, by virtue of an established set of alliances which had previously pitted *Kufuor, Obasanjo and Eyadéma against Rawlings and Abacha*. Rawlings's poor relations with Eyadéma were partly rooted in his periodic support for Gilchrist Olympio, son of the first Togolese president (whom Eyadéma once claimed to have killed) who had repeatedly tried to stand for president himself. Immediately after the Ghanaian polls closed, Rawlings sought solace with his only remaining friend in a presidential office, namely *Dénis Sassou Nguesso of the Republic of Congo*. On the anniversary of the 1967 coup in Togo, the Kufuor regime dispatched a high-level delegation and a military band to celebrate the event. Many independent observers, including the Centre for Democratic Development in Accra, criticised this open fraternisation with the *Eyadéma dictatorship* as both distasteful and in fundamental conflict with Kufuor's claims to be a champion of democracy. The government, for its part, argued that, at a time when negotiations between the Togolese government and the opposition parties seemed to be making some headway, it was important to play a constructive role. The fertile rumour mill suggested that Eyadéma was providing Kufuor with access to the '*juju*-men' whose magical charms had kept him in power for four decades. Viewers in the Volta region even claimed to have seen evidence of this in Togolese television coverage of Kufuor's visits to Eyadéma's home area. When a cameraman from the Ghana Broadcasting Corporation made the mistake of photographing and tape-recording some of the proceedings and then leaking them to the NDC, he was dismissed, provoking an uproar in Ghana.

In recognition of Ghana's singular contribution to international peacekeeping duties (29 missions over 40 years), the UN Secretary-General opened the Kofi Annan International Peacekeeping Training Centre in Accra to offer courses on subjects such as *conflict management, elections monitoring and peacekeeping operations.* The largest single contributor to the funding of the centre was the German government (€ 3.1 m), and its inauguration was delayed to enable Chancellor Gerhard Schröder to be present. Britain, Italy, Canada and the Netherlands promised to further increase the funding base over subsequent years.

In his capacity as ECOWAS chairman, Kufuor also hosted a special summit in March to draw up a plan of action for the funding of the infrastructural side of sub-regional integration. The *president of the World Bank, James Wolfensohn,* attended in person and confirmed financial backing for various projects to the tune of $ 4.9 bn. The summit also discussed the *NEPAD* initiative and inevitably came back to the issue of sub-regional conflict management.

The Ghana government's commitment has been symbolised in the operation of a separate Ministry of Regional Integration and NEPAD, with Dr. Kofi Apraku at its head. Within the sub-region, the Ghanaian authorities have been more inclined to implement ECOWAS agreements on the freedom of movement of people and goods than most of their neighbours. They have also been supportive of plans for launching a common West African currency, recognising the structural weakness of the cedi. However, progress on both fronts has been painfully slow.

Socioeconomic Developments

In his budget statement of 5 February, Minister of Finance Yaw Osafo-Maafo laid emphasis on consolidating the gains made over the previous year. In particular, the budget aimed at achieving a real GDP growth rate of 5.4%, a budget deficit of 1.7% of GDP and an inflation rate of below 10%. The regime continued to place its hopes on higher levels of inward private investment. In fulfilment of the NPP vision of a 'Golden Age of Business', Osafo-Maafo announced plans to reduce corporate income tax from 32.5% to 30%. Moreover, any new company that was listed on the Ghana stock exchange would qualify for a special reduced rate of 25%. The minister also made much of the fact that, having faithfully implemented the conditionalities under the *HIPC initiative* over the past three years, Ghana would benefit from substantial debt relief. Speaking publicly when the HIPC completion point was reached, Osafo-Maafo said that Ghana could expect to receive relief from $ 1.5 bn of bilateral and commercial debts and $ 100 m per year for 20 years from the multilateral agencies. The catch in HIPC was that the government was no longer free to borrow as before from the bilateral and multilateral agencies. Osafo-Maafo renewed the quest for financing from private sources, and not for the first time turned to companies whose business credentials seemed highly dubious. This provoked an uproar and the minister was forced to quietly withdraw from the proposed deal. In July, the limitations on ministerial power were underlined when Osafo-Maafo was forced to *rescind a promised salary increase* to public sector workers in response to IMF pressure. On 21 May, an agreement had been reached with the Ghana Civil Servants Association, the Ghana National Association of Teachers, the Ghana Registered Nurses Association and the Judicial Services Staff Association promising a 31% salary increase backdated to March. On 3 July, Osafo-Maafo was forced to write a letter to the managing director of the IMF outlining the background to the affair, his subsequent realisation that the increases would throw the budget out of balance and the decision to step away from the deal. The minister sought to create the impression of being transparent by releasing this letter to the press. However, it was more likely an attempt to demonstrate to union leaders, in what was after all an election year, that he had been prevented from carrying out his wishes by a power greater than himself.

The savings that were made under HIPC were expected to enable the government to channel greater resources into the fulfilment of its *Poverty Reduction Strategy Programme*. The government clearly sought to derive the maximum political effect from debt relief. Among the benefits of the HIPC initiative, for example, was the fact that the ministry of education was able to announce the upgrading of 31 secondary schools over the year. The HIPC brand was often placed on the buildings to drive home the point that government had been right all along. The government did not shy away from the need to mobilise more revenue internally, through new taxes and more efficient collection. Controversially, the NPP regime added 2.5% to value-added tax (raising the overall rate from 10 to 12.5%) in order to source the *Ghana Educational Trust Fund*, which was held to be the key to restoring the battered educational infrastructure of the country. The regime also launched a new White Paper, proposing significant reforms in the educational sector. The new set-up would consist of an eleven-year basic educational programme (between the ages of 4 and 15), to be followed by a four-year senior high school system. Students would be streamed according to their aptitude, to permit specialised training in vocational, technical, agricultural and general subjects, with apprenticeships held out as an alternative for those who did not enter the final cycle. The underlying rationale was that more Ghanaians would leave school with relevant practical qualifications.

In the health sector, the government insisted on the need for a properly resourced system, and tabled proposals for a *National Health Insurance Scheme* (NHIS) on 18 March. The idea here was that salaried employees would pay into the scheme at cedis 6,000 a month (the daily minimum wage being cedis 9,200 a day), while the districts would manage their own funds for non-wage earners. In his launch speech, President Kufuor expressed the view that it was unacceptable that 80% of cases of illness and death were easily preventable and pointed out that the NHIS would make it possible to address the main causes. However, treatment of *HIV/AIDS would be excluded* from the scheme, lest it overwhelm the budget. Apart from the cost of providing anti-retrovirals, a practical headache for the health authorities was the poaching of nurses by the British health service in particular, which the Blair government promised to address.

By the end of the year, the NPP regime was able to record some successes. The economy grew faster than projected, at 5.8%, even if inflation still stood at 11.8%. Although a slowing of foreign investment into Africa affected Ghana as well, there were some high-profile developments, most notably the *merger between Ashanti Goldfields and the South African giant, AngloGold*. This was expected to lead to larger investments in the gold mining sector. The government of Ghana, which had a stake of 17.2% in the old company, was to hold a stake of 3.4% in the new company, AngloGold Ashanti. Meanwhile, the mining lease at Obuasi in Ashanti region was to be extended to the year 2054. Another significant development was the merger between Guinness Ghana Ltd. and Ghana Breweries Ltd (owned by Heineken). Although the NPP regime was very keen to continue divesting the state of its stake in loss-making enterprises, it seriously considered buying out the bankrupt Kaiser Aluminium's 90% stake in the *Volta Aluminium Company* (VALCO). Ironically, this would also fulfil an earlier dream associated with Kwame Nkrumah – the nemesis of the Busia/Danquah tradition to which the NPP belongs – of owning the (shut-down) aluminium smelter. However, the development of the country's own bauxite resources remained as distant a prospect as ever. The *cocoa sector* continued to produce record export volumes, with an astonishingly high production figure of 700,000 metric tonnes being announced at the end of the season in July. NDC claimed that the government was reaping the fruits of their own agricultural policies, which was certainly true, given the time-lag between planting the trees and the first harvest. The cynics pointed out that the boom was also a sign of increased *smuggling* from Côte d'Ivoire. Indeed, Gbagbo himself complained that the Ghanaians were seeking to profit from the crisis in his country.

In the social sector, the year was dominated by blueprints rather than great success stories. However, the director of the *Ghana AIDS commission* noted that some headway had been made in the fight against HIV/AIDS. In 2004, the national rate of infection stood at 3.6%, with the eastern region (6.1%) being the worst and the northern region (2.1%) the least affected areas. Some 72,000 adults were estimated to have the AIDS virus. At the end of the year, it was suggested that Ghana would struggle to meet some of the Millennium Development Goals. In particular, it was questionable whether child mortality would fall to 78 lives per 100,000 live births and whether deaths from HIV/AIDS and malaria would start to decline in real terms. On a more positive note, primary school enrolment rates and the gender balance in education had both improved, as had access to potable water. Official statistics suggested a small dent was being made in the fight against poverty, but that there was a growing problem in the cities where *street children* have become a visible feature in recent years. What the authorities hoped to avoid was an influx of destitute refugees from across the border in Côte d'Ivoire.

Most Ghanaians considered that 2004 had been a good year. The country had mostly avoided the contagion of violence from the West African sub-region, had passed through a successful election process and even showed encouraging signs of economic progress. However, most Ghanaians were well aware that this could change if oil prices soared or if fighting in Côte d'Ivoire escalated.

Ghana in 2005

Paul Nugent

Although the ruling New Patriotic Party (NPP) enjoyed a safe majority in parliament, the performance of the government was subjected to closer critical scrutiny than at any other point since 2000. Claims of ministerial corruption recurred repeatedly over the course of the year. Whereas President J.A. Kufuor had hitherto been treated with considerable reverence by the media, he and his family also became the target of specific allegations. While the government often appeared rather embattled, it was greatly helped by the re-emergence of a deep rift within the opposition National Democratic Congress (NDC). There was also a modest uplift in the national economy over the year. Although this was not enough to make much visible impact on the lives of ordinary Ghanaians, it did at least enable ministers to claim that the stewardship of the country was in competent hands.

Domestic Politics

Under the constitution, the president is expected to give an account of his tenure at the end of each four-year term of office. Whereas his NDC predecessor as president, Jerry Rawlings, had not done so, Kufuor began the year with a *state of the nation* address to parliament on 4 January in which he robustly defended his first term (2000–04). He asserted that the economy was in much better shape than when he took over and reiterated his commitment to ensuring good governance and probity. The next four years were billed as Positive Change II, in which the president pledged to

 | DOI 10.1163/9789004308183_003

make greater strides towards achieving concrete results in poverty alleviation. While the NDC argued that Kufuor was claiming credit for many initiatives that had been started under Rawlings, independent commentators gave measured approval. Three days later, on 7 January, parliament itself was dissolved and the new one, chosen in the December 2004 elections and expanded from 200 to 230 members, was sworn in. The politicking began immediately when the NPP decided to drop the former speaker, who was then sponsored by the NDC instead. The NPP prevailed and later the same day, President Kufuor was sworn in for his second term.

The composition of the new *cabinet* became a matter of considerable public interest because it was taken as an indicator of who Kufuor might be backing to succeed him in 2008. The presidential nominations for ministerial posts produced few high-profile casualties. The highly regarded finance minister, Yaw Osafo Maafo, was moved to the education and sports portfolio. Although this would normally have been interpreted as a demotion, it was widely believed that Kufuor was manoeuvring him into a position where he might actually benefit from being the breaker of 'good news'. Qualification by the national football team for the World Cup finals in October was a turn of particularly good fortune. His replacement, Kwadwo Baah-Wiredu, was regarded as an equally safe pair of hands and in effect swapped ministries with Maafo. The parliamentary vetting of the president's nominees provoked much controversy when three prospective ministers were found to have misrepresented aspects of their personal histories and were accused being implicated in corruption. Once again, the NPP used its parliamentary majority to push the nominations through, to the intense annoyance of the NDC and the consternation of independent political commentators. At the start of June, it was revealed that one of the ministers in question, Dr. Richard Anane, was under investigation by the Commission for Human Rights and Administrative Justice (CHRAJ).

Former President *Rawlings* remained the most vocal and emotive critic of the NPP administration, accusing Kufuor of presiding over rampant corruption and abuse of office. He was pointedly out of the country at the time of the inauguration, and on 12 January he stated in a speech that the NDC could not afford to wait until 2008 to get rid of the NPP government. This was interpreted by the media as a coded call for the adoption of extra-constitutional means to oust Kufuor. When the University of Development Studies cancelled an event in which Rawlings was expected to receive an honorary doctorate in March, there were allegations that Vice-President Aliu Mahama had intervened to scupper the plans. This produced further accusations and counter-claims by spokesmen for the president and the former president. The efforts of church leaders and prominent chiefs to mediate yielded minimal results, and on 20 October Rawlings alleged that UN Secretary-General Kofi Annan was being used to bolster the image of the government. The Rawlings period remained in the public eye by virtue of the report of the *national reconciliation commission* which, among other things, recommended a referendum on the transitional provisions in the 1992 constitution that indemnified members of the PNDC regime (Provisional National Defence Council) from prosecution. Public commemoration of three high court judges and a retired military officer who were murdered in 1982, allegedly at the hands of those close to Rawlings, kept the revolutionary years in the public eye, as did the former president's public celebration of the anniversary of the '4 June Revolution'.

The government faced far more co-ordinated *opposition to liberalisation* reforms than had hitherto been seen. The single most contentious issue was deregulation of the petroleum sector. When petrol prices were raised on 18 February, the opposition parties joined forces in a Committee for Joint Action (CAJ) to rally the country in a series of rolling demonstrations. The first was held in Accra on 1 March and others followed across the regions over the course of the year. Critics of the increases argued that they were regressive and that they had been forced on Ghana by the IMF. The government retorted that subsidies were getting in the way of its capacity to finance other poverty alleviation initiatives. Rising prices on the world market forced government to increase prices on 8 August and again on 3 October, despite the political fall-out that was bound to ensue. The *privatisation* of utilities and state corporations was almost as contentious. In the case of the latter, there were allegations that members of the government were seeking to dispose of the Ghana Railways Corporation at rock-bottom prices in such a way as to benefit businessmen connected with the regime. The collapse of Ghana Airways and the creation of Ghana International Airlines as its successor were similarly depicted as asset-stripping. As far as utilities were concerned, attempts to privatise the management of urban water supplies were opposed by civil society groups. In March, when the multinational firm, Biwater, withdrew, this was claimed as a victory by the Coalition Against Water Privatisation.

The campaign in favour of more *equitable trade* gathered momentum. In April, when Juapong Textiles was reported to be in danger of closure, the secretary-general of the Textile, Garment and Leather Workers Union blamed the crisis in the industrial sector on dumping by foreign competitors, in particular China. Final closure of this flagship company followed in June. Ironically, the Nigerian authorities placed an embargo on Ghanaian imports, claiming that the country was being used as a conduit for smuggling dumped Chinese and European goods. Duties on imported rice and poultry also became the focus of public campaigns. In 2003, the government had proposed to increase duties on these items, but the enabling legislation was dropped for fear of alienating donors. The ministry of agriculture pointed out that the country only produced around 35% of its rice requirements and that any tariff increases would have to be borne by the consumer.

The minister of trade and industry did, however, promise tougher action to deal with smuggling and introduced a new requirement that textiles be imported through the Takoradi port only. The Coalition of Civil Society Organisations joined farmers' associations and trade unions in demanding greater *protection* for Ghanaian producers.

The issue of *corruption* dogged the government over the course of the year. A survey of popular perceptions conducted by the Ghana Integrity Initiative in four cities over March and April revealed that 90% of respondents believed corruption to be rife and that 60% perceived it as having worsened in recent years. In October, Transparency International placed Ghana 65th out of 159 countries on its corruption index, a slightly worse score than before. Despite Kufuor's repetition of his 'zero tolerance' policy, the media leaked a succession of rumours about high-level corruption, many of which appeared to be grounded in a modicum of fact. The president sacrificed some of the accused in order to demonstrate the seriousness with which he took the allegations. For example, senior officials in the energy commission were forced to step down on 6 May amid allegations that a vehicle had been bought for an Ashanti paramount chief. However, Kufuor seemed unwilling to act against members of his cabinet. Indeed, one independently minded NPP parliamentarian, P.C. Appiah-Ofori, claimed that whereas Rawlings had dealt swiftly with allegations of malfeasance, Kufuor was reluctant to act decisively.

In May, the revelation that a *son of the president*, 'Chief' John Kufuor, had been involved in the purchase of a partially built hotel near to his father's residence at a cost of $ 3 m led to allegations that he had merely been acting as a front man. Whereas the president denied any involvement and his son insisted that he was perfectly within his rights to engage in a business venture of his choosing, even the director of the non-partisan Centre for Democratic Development (CDD) voiced his concern that there appeared to be a cover-up. The media gave much publicity to the claim of a foreign national that she had been mandated by the president to negotiate the purchase of the hotel in 2001. Although CHRAJ promised an investigation, NDC spokesmen claimed that its acting head was a personal friend of the president and a former relation by marriage of an NPP minister. On 21 November, the 'Enquirer' newspaper reported Haruna Esseku, the NPP chairman, as complaining that the Castle (the presidential office) was pocketing kickbacks from government contracts that should have been going to the party instead. Although Esseku denied the story, a tape of the conversation appeared to substantiate the story. The serious fraud office promised an investigation. When the party held its congress on 17 December, Esseku quietly withdrew from the race, having become an object of vilification in the party. The year ended with the World Bank country director, Mats Karlsson, stating openly that corruption was "a real issue". The allegation that Kufuor's administration was deeply *nepotistic* also resurfaced, forcing the president on to the defensive. On 18 May, the president addressed members of the armed forces and pleaded that only two of his ministers were family members. His critics pointed out that the list of relatives heading public corporations and holding ambassadorial posts was much longer.

On the other side, the long-running case against members of the 31st December Women's Movement, who were alleged to have profited from divestiture of the Ghana Rubber Estates during the NDC years, collapsed. On 3 March, two former NDC ministers who had been *imprisoned* for causing financial loss to the state, Kwame Peprah and Victor Selormey, were amnestied by Kufuor, although the latter died shortly afterwards, renewing a debate about the parlous state of prison conditions.

The NPP continued to suffer from the fall-out from the assassination of the *Dagomba paramount chief* or Ya Na in 2002, which many people blamed on the government. The attempts to finally bury the Ya Na ran into serious problems with the factions associated with the Andani and Abudu chiefly lines. The Asantehene endeavoured to mediate, but was forced to suspend his efforts in April. On 4 November, the burial was postponed yet again for security reasons. In Greater Accra region, the swing against the NPP in the 2004 elections assumed a greater significance when a self-styled Ga Dangme Council, representing the interests of the Ga ethnic group who are indigenous to Accra, held demonstrations on 26 April to protest the alienation of Ga lands, despite a lack of backing from the Ga traditional council. This followed some years of grumbling by Ga nationalists about marginalisation of the indigenes as the capital city has expanded. In Kumasi, a group calling itself the Patriotic Citizens threatened its own demonstrations to protest against neglect of Ashanti interests.

In October, the NDC demanded that the NPP government drop a proposed piece of legislation, namely the Representation of the People (Amendment) Bill, which would enable Ghanaian *citizens resident abroad* to vote in national elections. The NDC regarded this as a brazen attempt to inflate the NPP share of the vote, given that people from Ashanti and the eastern region were disproportionately represented in the diaspora. The NPP position was that those living abroad made a very significant contribution through remittances and should therefore be rewarded with the franchise.

In the five *by-elections* that had been fought since 2000, the NPP had won all the contests with handsome majorities – even in NDC strongholds. Evidence that the tide had turned came with two by-elections. On 21 April, polling in the Kumasi seat of Asawase saw the NDC returned with an increased majority. The fact that this was a Muslim quarter of the city, containing many northern migrants, made the result understandable, but the NPP had believed that it was winnable. The second by-election took place in central Accra in Odododiodioo constituency and was similarly won by the NDC with an increased majority. The CDD criticised the excessive presence of security personnel and the sudden appearance of street lights and the tarring of roads in an attempt to influence voters. In November, the courts nullified the December results in Mion constituency and an NPP parliamentarian was arrested for drug trafficking in the United States, presenting the prospect of further by-elections in 2006.

Despite its excellent performance in these contests, the NDC squandered its advantage by engaging in an *internal power struggle*, in which Rawlings was pitted against the party chairman, Dr. Obed Asamoah. The latter stood accused of having undermined the electoral campaign of John Atta-Mills and Rawlings made no secret of his intention to remove the chairman and his supporters from office. The northern regional congress in September was marked by intimidation and bribery, which Rawlings blamed on the Asamoah faction. This set things up for a fight to the finish at the national congress on 22 December. Rawlings pulled out all the stops, with the result that Asamoah and his associates were roundly defeated. The first *resignations from the party* began almost immediately. Meanwhile, the Convention People's Party (CPP) and the People's National Convention (PNC), which had performed poorly in the 2004 elections, engaged in protracted negotiations with a view to a merger.

Foreign Affairs

On 19 January, Kufuor concluded his term as ECOWAS chairman, sparing himself possible embarrassment in relation to subsequent *developments in Togo*. Kufuor and President Eyadéma had been close allies despite the questionable democratic credentials of the latter. When Eyadéma died on 5 February and the military installed his son, Faure Gnassingbe, as his successor, there was pressure on ECOWAS member states to face down what was in effect a coup. The heads of state met in Niamey on 9 February, with Kufuor in attendance, and roundly condemned the military intervention. Upon his return, Kufuor and the foreign minister, Nana Akuffo-Addo, indicated that ECOWAS leaders were unanimous that pressure ought to be applied to secure a return to constitutional rule. However, there was much comment on the low profile of the Ghanaian president by comparison with his peers. The opposition parties insinuated that Kufuor was reluctant to take a stand against the son of his former ally. Akuffo-Addo replied that the president was active behind the scenes in seeking to bring about a peaceful resolution of the crisis. The agreement by Faure to step down and to abide by fresh elections was taken as vindication of a policy of quiet diplomacy and good neighbourliness. However, the violence that accompanied the subsequent election created problems when *refugees* spilled across the border, despite the official closure on the Togolese side. On 5 May, the immigration service reported that 12,933 refugees had been registered. The government was also embarrassed when shots fired by the Togolese military on 27 April injured three people in the border town of Aflao.

Two other developments turned border controls into a matter of increasing government concern. The first was the sudden arrival of refugees from Darfur through Togo in April. The second was the *armed incursions* by Ivorian rebels into Ghanaian territory, near Bole, on 12 March. The minister of defence was alarmed to discover that some Ghanaian soldiers appeared to be complicit, and swiftly recalled some of its peacekeepers in Côte d'Ivoire. The continuing crisis in that country remained a matter of serious concern and on 6 October, Kufuor held talks with President Chirac of France, which concentrated on joint measures to support the peace process. On 2 June, the arrest of what were originally thought to have been coup plotters turned out to be Togolese opposition supporters purchasing arms, which again underlined the security problems associated with the tribulations of neighbouring states.

The G8 summit in Gleneagles in July was the most important international event in a crowded calendar and President Kufuor attended in person. Ghana became the first country to submit itself to *peer review* under NEPAD. When the report was finally released in Abuja in June, it pointed to shortcomings as well as some achievements. It commented adversely on corruption and the quality of public service delivery and noted that Ghana was unlikely to meet the Millennium Development Goals. However, it also gave credit for the consolidation of democracy. Amid growing international criticism of NEPAD, President Kufuor failed to attend the NEPAD summit of heads of state in Egypt on 19 April, preferring instead to take part in an Afro-Asian summit in Jakarta, where he had the opportunity to meet with Chinese President Hu Jintao. During the Rawlings period, there had been significant Malaysian investment which the Kufuor administration regarded as tainted by association with the NDC regime. As a result, Ghana-Malaysia relations had become strained, as Kufuor openly admitted. One source of dispute concerned the termination of a stake by Telekom Malaysia in Ghana Telecom. On 8 May, the government of Ghana agreed to compensate the Malaysian company with a view to drawing a line under the affair. In mid-September, President Kufuor addressed the 60th session of the United Nations General Assembly where the Millennium Development Goals were under discussion. At this meeting, Ghana was elected to join the Security Council with effect from 2006.

On 6 April, the president travelled to Rome to attend the funeral of Pope John Paul II. In the same month, the charismatic *Brazilian president*, 'Lula' da Silva, arrived on a state visit from 12–14 April. This was the first visit by a Brazilian head of state, despite the historical ties between the countries. A joint chamber of commerce and a permanent joint commission of cooperation were inaugurated to promote closer economic and cultural links. On 26 October, Kufuor travelled to the United States on a visit to promote trade, investment and tourism and held a private meeting with President George W. Bush. This visit provoked a heated debate about the expenses incurred in the course of this constant presidential globetrotting.

Relations with the Gambia were strained after the mysterious deaths of 13 people believed to be Ghanaians seeking to emigrate illegally to Europe. While the Gambian media portrayed the deaths as the work of *human traffickers*, the Ghanaian authorities suspected the Gambian police. On 6 August, Akuffo Addo travelled to Banjul to register a formal complaint and demand an official enquiry.

Socioeconomic Developments

On 4 February, the outgoing finance minister reported that the economy was in better shape than at the start of his term. He indicated that the rate of GDP growth at the end of 2004 was 5.8%, slightly above the budgetary forecast. *Inflation* had come down from 40% to 11.8% and interest rates were lowered from 50% to 29%. The high cost of borrowing was a persistent source of complaint on the part of industry, alongside the high level of taxation. Having created a separate ministry for the private sector, the government promised to restore incentives.

This was an unusual year in which the country was presented with two budgets. On 24 February, Baah-Wiredu tabled his *2005 budget*, which lowered corporate taxation from 32.5% to 28% and reduced the national reconstruction levy, which had been criticised as a stealth tax. This was expected to give a boost to the industrial sector in particular. The Association of Ghanaian Industries welcomed the concessions, but insisted that the business environment remained unfriendly. Overall, the economy was projected to grow at 5.8% in 2005, while the fiscal deficit was expected to come down to 2.7%. On 10 November, the *budget for 2006* was read, having been brought forward in order to facilitate early disbursement of funds. Baah-Wiredu announced that the country was expected to meet its earlier growth target and to achieve a budget deficit of 2.4% of GDP for the year. The minister announced the commencement of the second phase of the Growth and Poverty Reduction Strategy (2006–09), in which the accent was to lie on job creation through the stimulation of private enterprise, in pursuit of which corporate tax was reduced still further to 25%. Support for the first year had been promised by the Consultative Group for Ghana the previous month, to the tune of $ 1.2 bn, enabling more money to be channelled into priority areas like education.

The most controversial measure was the decision to deregulate the *petroleum sector*. The highly indebted Tema oil refinery was henceforth to be limited to the processing of crude oil, while private companies would be encouraged to take over the importation of finished products. On 9 June, the construction of the West African gas pipeline project linking Nigeria, Benin, Togo and Ghana was formally commissioned. This was expected to relieve some of the pressures in energy supply.

The government estimate of how much *debt relief* Ghana was to receive under the HIPC initiative in 2005 was Cedis (¢) 1,992.9 bn, of which 398 bn was expected to go to domestic debt relief; 1,195 bn to sectoral programmes; 199 bn for distribution to district assemblies; and 199.3 bn was to be placed in a contingency fund. In June, the G8 finance ministers offered debt relief to 18 countries, with Ghana benefiting to the tune of $ 4.1 bn. Kufuor maintained that this was Ghana's reward for having opted for the rigours of the HIPC initiative. This was given reinforcement on 11 June when Kufuor and four other African heads of state were invited to the White House by President Bush, who praised them for their achievements. On 22 December, further good news became official when the IMF announced a total cancellation of all the debts incurred by Ghana prior to 2005, totalling some $ 381 m.

According to the Ghana Investment Promotion Centre, India surpassed Britain as the greatest source of foreign direct investment. With China in third place, the evidence pointed to the growing importance of Asian interests in Ghana. In April, a Chinese trade delegation visited the country to explore possible investments in areas such as textiles and electronics. The Kufuor regime committed itself to the *privatisation of the railways* and the renovation of the network, and looked to assistance from China and India. Whereas the colonially constructed railways stopped at Kumasi, the government signed a statement of intent with its counterpart, Burkina Faso, whereby the lines would be extended, enabling the latter to import its goods through Ghanaian ports. Running somewhat counter to the general trend was state involvement in the Volta Aluminium Company (VALCO). The latter had closed in 2002, but reopened in September after the Kaiser corporation sold its 90% stake to the state. On 11 July, Kufuor travelled to Jamaica, in part to explore the possibilities of using alumina from that country in an enlarged smelter. The president made much of the desire to reactivate Kwame Nkrumah's dream of an integrated aluminium industry, using bauxite mined at Kibi. Anglogold Ashanti, which owned the Obuasi gold mines as well as others in South Africa, had an indifferent year because the higher gold price was offset by rising fuel costs. In Obuasi, the mine management was accused by small-scale gold operators of intimidation, and on 21 July those in

Wassa took their complaint to CHRAJ. The volume of *cocoa* exports in 2004–05 was estimated by the Bank of Ghana to have fallen to 583,109 tonnes from 700,000 tonnes the previous year. The government made much of its pledge to improve the country's access to information technologies and to improve on its ranking by the World Economic Forum.

In September, the UNDP's Human Poverty Index listed Ghana at 62 out of 103 developing countries. Among all countries, it slipped from 131 to 138. The report noted that while the incidence of poverty was 2% in Accra, it was as high as 70% in the rural savanna. It also highlighted the failure of economic growth to trickle down in the manner the government had predicted. In the area of *health*, the government struggled to deal with an exodus of qualified nurses and doctors. It nevertheless pledged itself to greater efforts towards the eradication of guinea worm. In October and November, there was a cholera outbreak in Ashanti and the northern region, which stretched resources. The director of the AIDS Commission sparked a national debate by suggesting that prostitution be legalised in order to make it easier to fight the transmission of the disease. Although he received some support from bodies such as the Planned Parenthood Association, the government made it clear that it was reluctant to go down this road. The HIV/AIDS prevalence rates were reported to have dropped from 3.6% in 2003 to 3.1%, but with the eastern region continuing to report a rise. Parts of that region have historically accounted for many of the prostitutes in Accra, which could account for the higher incidence rates.

The minister of the interior estimated that there were some 3,000 people whose warrants for arrest had expired, but who remained in prison. The justice system struggled to cope with the numbers, as did the prisons. Hence, on 4 March, President

Kufuor released 1,347 prisoners on humanitarian grounds to mark independence celebrations. In a speech to mark international literacy day on 8 September, Osafo-Maafo drew attention to the fact that as much as 47% of the population (or seven million people) remained *illiterate*, despite the strides that had been made since 1984. In this case, the worst figures were to be found in the north and among women. In 2005, the government pushed ahead with plans to introduce free and compulsory universal basic education.

Ghana in 2006

Paul Nugent

There were encouraging signs that economic growth was gathering momentum. The International Development Association of the World Bank was among those that saw Ghana as the emerging success story in Africa, stating that the country was on track to achieve middle-income status by 2015. The government actively continued to offer inducements to the private sector and solicited additional aid from East Asia, specifically China, for telecommunications and infrastructural development. On the political front, all eyes were fixed on the campaign for leadership of the two leading parties, the New Patriotic Party (NPP) and the National Democratic Congress (NDC), as the 2008 elections loomed. The main parties traded accusations about their respective records of involvement in corruption and drug trafficking, while the smaller parties struggled to set an agenda of their own.

Domestic Politics

There were five issues that dominated politics over the course of the year. The most hotly debated in the early months was the passage of the Representation of the People (Amendment) Act or ROPAA. The government maintained that Ghanaians in the *diaspora*, who contributed so much through remittances (allegedly 14.4% of GDP in 2005), should enjoy the right to vote with effect from 2008. The NDC was opposed, for the reason that the NPP had its greatest concentration of support in the Akan areas that accounted for the greater part of the Ghanaian community

 | DOI 10.1163/9789004308183_004

abroad. It therefore seemed as if the NPP was seeking to alter the rules of the game to its advantage. The minority leader in parliament, Alban Bagbin, avoided making this point on the floor of the house on 2 February, resorting instead to a catalogue of inconsistencies in the government case. He highlighted the difficulties the electoral commission would face in verifying who had the right to vote. However, his deputy's attempts to secure a legal writ restraining the Speaker from permitting further readings failed on 6 February. Three days later, the NDC started a *boycott of parliament*. The other opposition parties were divided. Within the People's National Convention (PNC), John Ndebugre supported ROPAA and was suspended from the vice-chairmanship of the party for doing so. On 14 February, the parties opposed to the legislation, united under the banner of Concerned Citizens, took to the streets of Accra to demonstrate in the first of a series of rolling protests. However, the government passed ROPAA on 23 February. Having lost this battle, the NDC returned to parliament on 2 March, hoping that it might still win the war.

The second salient issue was that of *corruption*, which had become a matter of concern during the previous year. The president reiterated his stance of 'zero tolerance' and on 27 July the Whistleblower Bill was finally passed, enabling individuals to disclose malpractices in the public interest. Nevertheless, the opposition and some newspapers alleged that graft was endemic at all levels of government. The annual Transparency International ratings placed Ghana 70th out of 163 countries in terms of perceptions of corruption. The country-specific index indicated that such perceptions had returned to where they had been in the last year of the NDC administration. To impartial observers, that sounded about right. The allegations that had been levelled in 2005 against Dr. Richard Anane, the roads transport minister, were investigated by the Commission on Human Rights and

Administrative Justice (CHRAJ) through a series of public hearings. His former mistress, and mother of his illegitimate child, gave evidence in camera by satellite linkup. She claimed that she had been advised that it would be unsafe to come to Ghana to testify. She confirmed that she and Anane had conspired to use kickbacks to pay for the upkeep of their son, and that she had only decided to blow the whistle when Anane had stopped returning calls. To the consternation of many, Anane was not sacked in the April cabinet reshuffle. However, on 15 September, CHRAJ recommended his dismissal on grounds of conflict of interest, perjury and abuse of power, even though there was insufficient evidence to establish actual corruption. On 2 October, Anane reluctantly resigned. On 4 May, CHRAJ also issued its report on preliminary investigations into allegations of corruption and *conflict of interest* made against President Kufuor. These related to the purchase of a hotel by his son. CHRAJ declared that there was no evidence to suggest that the president was a stakeholder, although many critics pointed out that the foreign woman who had implicated Kufuor had not been given a similar chance to testify.

Members of parliament have relatively few chances for enrichment, but on 28 March the Ghana Aids Commission claimed that 122 MPs who had received money for HIV/AIDS campaigns had failed to account for the money. On 23 March, it was announced that MPs would in future no longer have direct access to their share of the district assemblies' common funds for local development projects, but would have to pass through the district chief executives in order to *minimise abuses*. This coincided with a dispute in Abuakwa South constituency where the foreign minister, Nana Akuffo-Addo, reacted to claims that executives had misdirected money from the common fund by demanding an audit. An enquiry later exonerated the officials.

The chief justice was himself accused of abuse of office and an inquiry was instigated by the president on the basis of a specific allegation. But on 13 July, the supreme court ruled that the president's intervention had been unconstitutional. Meanwhile, the vendetta against the former NDC government continued. On 12 April, the former first lady, Nana Agyeman Rawlings, and a number of senior ex-officials were put before the Fast Track Court for causing financial loss to the state. This related to the divestiture of the Nsawam cannery. The NDC sought to turn the tables whenever it could. On 26 May, work began on the construction of a new presidential palace and questions were soon raised about monitoring of expenditure. At the same time, the ministry of defence became embroiled in a public row over the exchange of the presidential jet, which had been purchased by the previous NDC regime, in return for military aircraft.

The third issue, which dominated the second half of the year, was a series of *cocaine* seizures, indicating that Ghana had become a transit country for hard drugs. Even more worrying was the evidence that government officials were implicated. This unfolded against the backdrop of the trial of an NPP parliamentarian in the US for cocaine trafficking. Following the discovery that a haul of 2,300 tonnes of cocaine had mysteriously disappeared from a vessel that docked at Tema harbour and the disclosure of a taped discussion between a senior police officer and alleged traffickers over the whereabouts of the drugs, the Justice Georgina Wood inquiry was set up in July. There were many calls for the inspector-general of police, Patrick Akyeampong, to be dismissed and hard questions were asked about immigration procedures at the airport when it transpired that there were incomplete records of the movement of suspected traffickers. Meanwhile, five 'drug barons' were put on trial. Kufuor tried to deflect the blame on to the NDC, claiming that the *Venezuelan traffickers* had been brought to Ghana by a stalwart of the former government, Robert Mettle-Nunoo. On 8 September, his assets and those of a number of people whose names cropped up in the Wood inquiry were frozen by the serious fraud office. But bizarrely, the question at issue was whether they had paid their taxes. Even more controversially, someone from the Asantehene's palace was mentioned on the tape, leading the king to fulminate against tribally motivated attacks against the Ashantis. On 25 November, the relevant minister, Albert Kan-Dapaah, declared that the police inspector-general would not be sacked, while the legal case against the accused began to implode.

The fourth issue concerned the *burial* of the *Ya Na*, the king of Dagomba (who had been murdered by the rival Abudu faction in 2002) and the appointment of a successor. On 18 March, the Abudus promised to cooperate with the Andanis in ensuring that the Ya Na was properly buried, but with conditions attached, notably their refusal to accept the appointment of a regent. This provoked a vigorous riposte from the Andanis on 28 March, just as the Tamale Central by-election was starting to heat up. However, on 1 April a mediating committee of eminent kings, headed by the Asantehene, announced an accord that seemed to have satisfied both parties, thereby permitting the burial to go ahead nine days later. On 21 April, an Andani regent and acting Ya Na was peacefully installed, but on 25 August there was a clash between the two sides that led to fatalities in Yendi, suggesting that this dispute was not yet over.

Finally, this was a year in which Ghanaians woke up to the realisation that they would be electing someone to replace Kufuor in 2008. Covert *campaigning* for the succession within the NPP gathered pace. Some argued that the eastern region's turn was overdue. The names that were touted as possible candidates included that of Yaw Osafo-Maafo, whose movement from finance to the education and sports ministry after the 2004 elections was deemed fortuitous because of unfolding good-news stories. The other key name was that of Akuffo-Addo. On 15 March, the 'Statesman' newspaper (founded by the latter) noted that the failure to fix a date for the leadership contest was creating unnecessary uncertainty. Among the non-easterners, the president's own brother, Kwame Addo-Kufuor, recurred in press reports about undercover campaigning. However, this was doubly problematic for the NPP because it would involve both an Ashanti and a *dynastic succession* that was bound to be unpopular in the country at large. As the only northerner in the race, Vice-President Aliu Mahama used the facilities that his office afforded him to maximum effect.

The president allegedly had to warn his cabinet colleagues on more than one occasion of the fact that they all had jobs to perform. On 28 April, Kufuor embarked on a major *cabinet reshuffle*, justified in terms of 'downsizing'. Several prominent ministers were dropped, among them Osafo-Maafo. Kofi Apraku's ministry of regional co-peration and NEPAD was subsumed under Akuffo-Addo's portfolio, with the result that Apraku, too, lost his job. By June, the lobbying of groups calling themselves 'Friends of Akuffo-Addo' and 'Friends of Kofi Konadu Apraku' was a clear indication that the leadership campaign had begun in earnest. On 25 July, Akuffo-Addo finally made his intentions explicit in the course of a canvassing tour in the Upper East, followed by Kwame Addo-Kufuor on 5 August. However, the choice of candidate was not expected to take place until well into 2007.

Following a rancorous NDC convention at Kororidua in December, at which Dr. Obed Asamoah was ousted as national chairman, the man who had effectively founded the party resigned on 5 January citing 'violence and hooliganism' by Rawlings supporters. A few days later, Asamoah announced the formation of a Democratic Freedom Party, which proceeded to win endorsements from some prominent ex-NDC stalwarts in the Volta region. Asamoah's exit left Jerry Rawlings firmly in control of the NDC, even if *ongoing resignations* threatened to damage the party's future prospects. A prominent defection to the NPP came in early January when Wayo Seini, who had previously accused the government of complicity in the murder of the Ya Na, resigned his NDC parliamentary seat. He announced his intention to rejoin the NPP. However, his application could not be processed in time for the Tamale Central *by-election*, forcing him to contest it as an independent. The NPP decided not to put up a candidate, citing tensions in Dagomba, and gave a belated endorsement to Seini. However, the by-election was comfortably won by the NDC with 68% of the vote, making it three out of three wins since the 2004 polls.

On 24 October, the NPP comfortably retained the Offinso South seat (Ashanti) in a by-election, breaking its apparent jinx. However, the reality remained that the NDC was a force to be reckoned with and that lent added significance to the leadership question. Dr. Ekwow Spio-Garbrah, a former Rawlings minister, made the early running and was widely seen as the most serious challenger to John Atta-Mills. The only others to file nominations were Alhaji Mahama Iddrisu, also a former minister, and Eddie Annan, a businessman. On 21 December, the NDC party congress met to choose its candidate. On this occasion, Rawlings refrained from backing anyone explicitly. However, this did not prevent Mills from winning by a very large margin. The other candidates accepted defeat graciously and the party celebrated its *new-found unity*.

On 23 October, the cold war between Kufuor and Rawlings heated up again when the president accused his predecessor of soliciting funds from an oil-rich country to destabilise the government. The press took this to be a reference to the Venezuelan president, Hugo Chavez, whereas Rawlings thought it was a reference to the Middle East. On 26 September, the country went to the polls to elect unit committees and district assembly members. The candidates stood on individual non-party platforms as before, which made it an unhelpful guide as to the strength of the parties.

In February, alleged government plans to remove the preventive aspects from the Customs, Excise and Preventive Service

(CEPS) and to reallocate them to the Ghana Immigration Service (GIS) caused ripples of open dissent in CEPS. On 15 February, the government denied that CEPS would lose any of its existing functions or undergo retrenchment. But when on 16 July, Minister of Interior Albert Kan Dapaah announced that a sum of Cedis 1.9 bn was being allocated to a border control programme – to deal with smuggling, human trafficking, passport fraud and cross-border crime – the task of implementation was allotted to the GIS. The latter would set up a border patrol unit that clearly encroached on CEPS terrain.

Finally, there was one issue on which Ghanaians were united and that was the pride that the national team, the 'Black Stars', instilled at the *World Cup finals* in Germany. A decisive defeat at the hands of Italy, the eventual winners, dampened hopes, but clear wins against the Czech Republic and the US put Ghana into the knockout stages. Although Ghana lost to Brazil on 27 June, team members were hailed as returning heroes and provided with national medals on 3 July.

Foreign Affairs

Ghana took up a *non-permanent seat* at the UN Security Council and in August it served as the rotating chair. This gave an enhanced profile to President Kufuor. On 1 May, Japanese Prime Minister Koizumi arrived on a state visit to drum up support for a permanent Japanese seat.

Kufuor has been criticised for the excessive number of foreign trips he has made and, if anything, these increased in 2006. The primary focus was East Asia, which the government regarded as the most likely source of concessionary aid. On 19 June, Chinese Prime Minister Wen Jiabao arrived in Ghana on a two-day visit. In return for various trade and aid deals, the government issued a communiqué stating Ghana's support for a united *China*. A Chinese business delegation followed in short order, promising to make Ghana the conduit for Chinese cars to the sub-region. On 2 November, Kufuor arrived in Beijing for the third Sino-African summit. On arrival, he repeated his wish that the Chinese assist with the construction of the Bui dam, rural electrification and telecommunications. Wen Jiabao promised that China would buy more processed goods from Ghana. But the reality was that by 2006, China was the second largest exporter to the country. Chinese companies were also awarded a number of high-profile contracts. Construction of the Sekondi sports stadium, to be completed in time for the 2008 African Nations Cup, ran into controversy when the 'Ghanaian Chronicle' alleged on 8 February that Chinese convict workers were used while local youth were ignored.

While courting China, the government also sought to make the most of its favourable image in Washington. President Bush invited Kufuor to visit in early April. Their joint press appearance emphasised Ghana's reward for good governance in the form of disbursements under the *Millennium Challenge Account*. A grant of $ 547 m was approved for a five-year programme targeted at poverty eradication and development interventions in the rural sector. The social projects were expected to cover water, sanitation and electricity ($ 100 m), while the agricultural development component ($ 240 m) would assist farmers with access to credit and promote land reform. A further $ 143 m would be channelled into infrastructural improvements. However, the list of regions that were expected to benefit excluded Upper East and Upper West, which were manifestly the poorest of all. Rather implausibly, the president claimed that 2 m new jobs would be created.

At the start of June, the president embarked on a foreign tour that took in the US, the UK, Nigeria and a visit to the football World Cup finals in Germany. The fact that his absence coincided with a strike by doctors, health workers and teachers provoked some adverse comment. On 4 July, having just returned from an AU summit in Banjul, he left for a state visit to Brazil with a stop-off in Britain. This was reckoned to be his 31st foreign visit in 18 months, provoking renewed press complaints about the expense of such *presidential globetrotting*. More was to come. In July, Kufuor travelled to Liberia for the independence celebrations before flying back to Washington for the signing of the Millennium Challenge Account agreement on the 28th. On 12 September, he flew to Cuba to attend a summit of the Non-Aligned Movement and on 15 October he left again for Italy. He then rounded up the year with a state visit to Mali.

The African dimension of Ghana's diplomacy concentrated mostly on cementing peace in neighbouring *Côte d'Ivoire*. On 5 July, Nana Akuffo-Addo attended a meeting in Yamoussoukro chaired by Kofi Annan and attended by a number of heads of state. Ghana also sought to bolster the fledgling Liberian government. Whereas the Togo front was quiet, relations with Burkina Faso improved greatly. On 11 March, the Ghana-Burkina Faso permanent commission for cooperation met in Ougadougou to advance cooperation on a number of fronts, including border demarcation, which AU states are supposed to have completed by 2012. Akuffo-Addo conceded that progress on closer cooperation had been slow, but claimed that the Kufuor years had brought renewed urgency. On 2 April, a meeting between the Upper East administration and its Burkinabè counterpart ensued at which it was agreed that the number of checkpoints should be decreased to facilitate freedom of movement. In June, the newly elected Benin president, Yayi Boni, visited the country. Here again, the presidents agreed on the need to reduce customs and immigration restrictions and the importance of binding together Ghana, Togo, Benin and Nigeria, which would soon be linked by a new gas pipeline and an improved coastal road. On 28 September, Ghana joined the *Francophonie* group of countries, to the surprise of many.

Socioeconomic Developments

The current population of Ghana was estimated at 19 m, with an average growth rate of 3%. With Greater Accra growing at 4.4% and the poorer northern regions coming in at significantly below the national average, the pace of *urbanisation* was very apparent. The phenomenon of street children was regarded as a growing problem in Accra and Kumasi. The trafficking of children, within and across borders, also received growing publicity.

The Growth and Poverty Reduction Strategy II Report (GPRS II, 2006–09) was debated in parliament in March, with a number of MPs claiming that cost recovery was contributing to impoverishment in rural areas. However, on 4 September the IMF claimed that Ghana was making such strides that it might halve *poverty* by 2012, three years ahead of the deadline set under the Millennium Development Goals. However, the HDI, released on 10 November, placed the achievements in context. The report ranked Ghana 136th in the world out of 177 countries. It estimated life expectancy at birth at 57 years and the adult literacy rate at 57.9%. Those without access to improved water stood at 25%.

On 19 January, the deputy minister for *health*, Samuel Owusu-Agyei admitted that the projected coverage of 50% for the national health insurance scheme had not been met in 2005. The actual figure was 30%, but he said he expected the figure to rise to 55% in 2007. The brain drain remained a problem, with almost as many Ghanaian doctors residing in the US as were working in Ghana. Whereas WHO recommended one doctor per 5,000 people, the figure in Ghana was one per 11,000.

Under the education sector plan (2003–15), the government remained committed to free universal primary *education* by 2015 and made a start by abolishing a range of school charges. Although education through the first nine years is supposed to be compulsory, the figures for 2005 suggested the enrolment was 87.5% at the primary level (90.5% boys and 84.4% girls), falling to 72.8% for junior secondary school (77.3% boys and 68.1% girls).

In August, the question of whether *homosexuality* should be legalised came to the fore when the president of the gay and lesbian association of Ghana took to the airwaves to present its case. Minister of Information and National Orientation Kwamena Bartels insisted that there would be no change to the law.

The government received praise for its handling of the economy, but questions were raised about whether the regime was really committed to its 'Golden Age of Business'. The state actually reasserted its control over the two fixed telephone companies (Ghana Telecom and Westel). However, the real expansion was in mobile phone uptake, with 2.6 m subscribers, of whom 60% belonged to the Areeba network. On 7 August, the minister of communications, Mike Oquaye, announced that the government intended to dispose of the majority of the shares in Ghana Telecom once again. More symptomatic was the crisis in the *aviation industry*. Against the backdrop of the withdrawal of South African Airways to Dakar, a struggle for control of Ghana International Airlines (GIA) – the former national airline that is 70% state-owned – became symptomatic of government interference. On 7 April, the presidential chief of staff, Kwadwo Mpianim, acted on a decision to dismiss the GIA management by sending security personnel to lock out the chief executive. He, in turn, complained to the American embassy. The vice-president of GIA, Sammy Crabbe, who happened to be the Greater Accra regional chairman of the NPP, mobilised his own party associates to defend the GIA offices. This was all deeply embarrassing, not least because it happened as Kufuor was in Washington at the invitation of President Bush. The Centre for Democratic Development (an independent think-tank) criticised the lack of transparency surrounding the creation of GIA as well as the manner in which positions had been filled. In

October, the American partner company took the Ghana government to the international court of arbitration in the Hague.

Again, the government's commitment to free markets wavered in relation to the *textile industry*, where cheap Chinese imports wreaked havoc. The government's ruling that all textile imports should pass through Takoradi port brought the phenomenon of overland smuggling through Togo into sharp relief. Kufuor committed the regime to the reopening of Juapong Textiles, which had closed in 2005 due to financial losses. Indeed, more money from the Presidential Special Initiative was channelled into the garments sector, in the belief that Ghana could export to Europe and North America.

The government did seek to allow market forces to determine the domestic price for *petroleum*. Prices increased by 32.6% over the first seven months of the year, providing the Committee for Joint Action, a united front of opposition politicians, with the chance to widen the scope of its public protests. But the government insisted that it had no option but to pass on rising prices on the global market. However, after a rise in July, it announced the abolition of the 15% ad valorem tax on petroleum in order to bring pump prices back down a bit. This was not as profound as it sounded because the government found other ways of taxing petroleum. However, lower global prices made it possible to reduce the pump price on 25 September.

On 27 March, Dr. Paul Acquah, governor of the Bank of Ghana, predicted that the rate of *inflation* would fall to single-digit levels by December, despite higher fuel prices. The statistical service reported that this had indeed been achieved in the month of March, but a 20% public sector wage increase alongside a swingeing petrol price hike at the start of May, and again on 20 July, had an inevitable inflationary effect.

On 13 July, Minister of Finance Kwadwo Baah-Wiredu put a supplementary budget before parliament. This amounted to requesting areas of additional expenditure to cover aspects of GPRS II. The minister promised further improvements in *revenue collection.* He explained that a higher budget deficit in the first four months of the year was no cause for alarm because the spending year now began from January.

On 15 November, in advance of the 2007 budget reading, the Ghana statistical service declared that the *GDP growth* rate for the current year was estimated at 6.2%. When Baah-Wiredu introduced the budget the next day, he cited this figure as vindication for the claim that the economy was robust. His figure for industrial growth was 7.3%, but agriculture grew at 5.9%, below the target of 6.6%. The minister also stated that inflation stood at 10.5% at the end of October. Baah-Wiredu was explicit about the search for new sources of development assistance. He said that $ 482 m had been raised by the end of September, of which 65% came from multilateral institutions. The minister noted that the total public debt had declined from $ 8.4 bn in 2005 to $ 4.8 bn in September 2006, largely due to *debt cancellations.* The projections for 2007 included a 6.5% GDP growth rate and single digit inflation. Baah-Wiredu also claimed that Ghana would no longer require IMF loans but would enter the international capital market. The NDC claimed that the figures did not add up. Most sectors had registered growth rates below the projected targets. Baah-Wiredu had attributed the countervailing gains to rapid expansion in the water and electricity sub-sectors, but low water levels in the Volta lake had necessitated a spell of power-cuts and water shortages. Although the NDC questioning of the figures sounded plausible, international financial institutions vindicated government claims about a vibrant economy that was starting to make a dent on unemployment and poverty. Hence, the poverty headcount index was estimated by the IDA to have fallen from 42% in 2001 to 32% in 2005.

Ghana in 2007

Paul Nugent

The focal point of public discourse was the celebration of the 50th anniversary of independence on 6 March, which provided an occasion for refl ection on what had been achieved and indeed whether there was anything worthy of celebration. Once the festivities were concluded, attention focused on the choice of candidates to lead the respective parties into the next election. The battle to succeed President J.A. Kufuor as leader of the New Patriotic Party (NPP) was particularly intense. All of this took place against the backdrop of a crippling energy crisis, the responsibility for which became perhaps the most hotly debated issue. As far as the economy was concerned, the power cuts, which were a consequence of the low water levels in the Volta lake, were ironically compounded by severe fl ooding in September. While the fi rst took its toll on industry, the second led to falling levels of agricultural production. Although donors remained upbeat, economic targets were not met.

Domestic Politics

The year-long festivities to mark the *independence anniversary*, carried out under the 'Ghana@50' logo, became acutely contentious at the start of the year. On 26 January, the minority leader in parliament, Alban Bagbin, complained that non-NPP supporters had been excluded from the organisation. In an attempt to defuse some of the criticism, a delegation of eminent persons was despatched by Kufuor to former President Jerry Rawlings on 15

 | DOI 10.1163/9789004308183_005

February to invite him to attend the celebrations in person. On 3 March, Rawlings finally issued a public statement to the effect that he could not in all conscience attend in view of "pervasive corruption at all levels, missed opportunities for genuine progress, nepotism, tribalism and known cases of political torture and killings".

The person in charge of 'Ghana@50', Dr. Charles Wereko-Brobby, was a controversial appointment, having been removed as chief executive of the Volta River Authority (VRA) in 2003 for under-performance (he was still fighting in the courts for compensation in February). Wereko-Brobby infuriated MPs when he refused to appear before the public accounts committee on 21 February to account for the *spending* of the $ 20 m that had been set aside for the celebrations. This followed concerns raised on the floor of parliament by Dr. Paa Kwesi Nduom, the minister for public sector reform. Wereko-Brobby accused Nduom of having brought about his downfall at the VRA and blamed him in part for the energy crisis. The chief of staff and minister for presidential affairs, Kwadwo Mpiani, had to step in to deal with parliamentary questions, but when he was unable to give a detailed account of expenditure, he was taken to task by irate MPs. Serious questions were raised about the use of the funds. In a speech on 14 February, Bagbin claimed that "contracts are flying like confetti to cronies and other party apparatchiks and hangers-on". The revelation that the organisers had ordered the commemorative cloth from China rather than supporting local industries created a storm of protest among manufacturers, trade unions and other critics of the government. The controversy took a further twist when on Independence Day Kufuor chose to wear a dull grey suit rather than a kente cloth.

The festivities passed off without incident, and were attended by many dignitaries, including eight African heads of state.

Despite early indications that the National Democratic Congress (NDC) would follow Rawlings in *boycotting* proceedings, the party agreed to take part. John Atta-Mills, the NDC leader, was among those at the parade ground. But the fact was that Bagbin provided a renewed source of grievance. Kufuor made a speech that managed to praise both Nkrumah and his associates and members of the Busia/Danquah tradition. The list of heroes tactfully included people from all regions of the country.

On 23 January, the NPP continued to recover from its lacklustre form in *by-elections* by retaining the safe Fomena seat. A more interesting contest was set up when Nkoranza North fell vacant after the sitting MP was charged with drug smuggling in the US. This had been an NDC seat until 2004 and the party hoped to recapture it. On 13 March, the NPP retained the seat comfortably, although the NDC complained of voter intimidation. As nominations for the choice of parliamentary candidates to contest the 2008 elections loomed, the NPP witnessed serious in-fighting within the constituencies. In Greater Accra, two MPs were suspended from attending constituency meetings because of their alleged intimidation of executive members.

From the second quarter of the year the race for the *NPP nomination* intensified. The brother of the president, Kwame Addo-Kufuor, signalled his intention to stand, but Kufuor pointedly refused to back him. To have done so would have invited charges of dynastic ambition. Kufuor was believed to strongly favour Alan Kyerematen, although he repeatedly denied it. Kyerematen was partly Fante by origin, thereby avoiding the equally explosive charge that Kufuor was engineering an Ashanti succession. But the passage was less than smooth. Kyerematen became embroiled in controversy over his management of the ministry of trade, industry and private sector development. A petitioner to the Commission on Human Rights and Administrative Justice

(CHRAJ) alleged conflicts of interest and the improper use of funds. Although Kyerematen was exonerated, the suggestion that his record was patchy provided ammunition for his opponents. On 12 June, seven NPP ministers were told that they should resign their ministerial positions in view of their intention to participate in the contest for the leadership. Nduom of the Convention People's Party (CPP) was forced to resign as well when it became clear that he intended to stand for the nomination of his own party.

In the last quarter of the year, the gloves came off as no fewer than 18 candidates traded accusations and toured the country drumming up support. Kyerematen, popularly dubbed 'Alan Cash', played on his personal wealth and largesse. His main rival, Nana Akuffo-Addo, emphasised his political experience, but even he was reported to have made significant 'donations' to potential delegates. As the owner of the 'Statesman' newspaper, Akuffo-Addo enjoyed a particular advantage. On 23 December, the NPP held its *congress*. One candidate was debarred from standing at the last minute because he had misled the party about his previous conviction for mutiny while in the armed forces. The election was won comfortably by Akuffo-Addo with 47.9% of the delegate vote, followed by Kyerematen with 32.5%. The hapless vice president, Aliu Mahama, came in third with 6.3%, but that was significantly better than Addo-Kufuor, who garnered only 1% of the delegate votes. Mahama announced his retirement from active politics, while the other defeated candidates rallied behind Akuffo-Addo. The exception was Kyerematen, who later complained of intimidation.

The CPP hoped to cash in on the independence anniversary, reminding Ghanaians on more than one occasion that it was Nkrumah that had brought independence and the Busia/Danquah tradition that had attempted to apply the brakes. But the CPP remained deeply divided, in particular over the participation of Nduom in the government. However, the latter was the clear winner in the race to lead the party when the delegates met on 17 December, and the CPP seemed to recover some confidence. On 2 December, Edward Mahama was chosen for the third successive time as the presidential candidate of the People's National Convention (PNC). The NDC had already selected Atta-Mills in 2006.

Relations between the government and the NDC took a turn for the worse on 5 February when a former Rawlings minister and sitting MP, Dan Abodakpi, was sentenced to a ten-year prison sentence for having caused financial loss to the state. His co-defendant, Victor Selormey, had previously died in custody. The NDC held a press conference the following day during which it alleged that the trial had been politically motivated and that the judgment was faulty. The NDC immediately began a boycott of parliament, which lasted until 19 February. In July, Ghanaians came to hear of a court case in Norway in which an employee of the Scancem cement company, who was accused of stealing company funds, alleged that the money had been used to *bribe* members of the previous government, including Rawlings, Mrs. Rawlings and P.V. Obeng, who was a longstanding member of the Rawlings government in the 1980s. The NPP press jumped on the story, but the charges were never substantiated. What did emerge, however, was evidence that Ghacem, the Ghanaian subsidiary that controlled the domestic cement factory, paid money to both of the political parties before elections.

The issue of *corruption* remained a contentious one. The campaign for probity received a body blow when the findings against a former minister, Dr. Richard Anane, were overturned by the Fast Track Court. The basis was not that the initial judgment was wrong, but that CHRAJ had exceeded its powers. The judgment was upheld by the supreme court, which ruled that CHRAJ was not entitled to initiate investigations on the basis of media allegations, but was required to wait for formal complaints to be made to it. Anti-corruption campaigners regarded this as an extremely retrograde step that would hamper the efforts of anti-corruption agencies.

The 2006 report on human rights practices issued by the US State Department, was critical of deaths resulting from the excessive use of force and vigilante justice. This became an issue in 2007 after the policing of *chieftaincy disputes* culminated in casualties. Although the 1992 constitution supposedly insulated chieftaincy from political interference, the NPP was accused of meddling in succession disputes. On 14 April, a new Ga Mantse was enstooled under the title of King Tackie Tawiah III at a ceremony attended by three ministers. Many Ga maintained that the individual had no rightful claim. On 1 November, there was an outbreak of violence at Anloga, which left one policeman and five civilians dead. The spark was an attempt to enstool the regent of Anlo as the substantive Awoamefia (or paramount chief). The Fast Track Court had ruled against the installation at the last minute, following an application by the attorney-general, but the installation had proceeded anyway. The government, which imposed a curfew after the clash, was widely blamed because the police had been sent to assist with the enstoolment. The regional minister was at the centre of these allegations of interference. Rawlings waded in and accused Kufuor of trying for political reasons to impose a candidate who had no traditional claim to the stool.

During April, speculation that the US wished to establish a *military base* in Ghana provoked a vigorous public debate. Addo-Kufuor, the minister of defence, repeatedly denied that any such plans existed, but on 23 April the State Department reported that the Pentagon would make a decision about the location of the projected Africa Command in October. Ghana was apparently being considered as a possible candidate.

On 21 March, one of the great independent voices in Ghanaian politics was silenced when Hawa Yakubu, a former MP, died. She was followed four days later by the chief justice, George Kingsley Acquah. The latter was replaced by a woman, Georgina Wood, in early June. On 31 May, the former wife of Kwame Nkrumah, Fathia, died in Cairo. Her body was returned to Ghana for a *state burial.*

Foreign Affairs

On 27 January, President Kufuor attended the eighth extraordinary session of the AU in Addis Ababa. Despite a strong bid by the Sudanese head of state, Kufuor was elected *president* of the *AU assembly*. The crisis in Darfur, in which the Sudanese government was believed to be complicit, kept Kufuor busy for much of the year. At the same meeting, Ghana tabled its responses to the recommendations of the African peer review panel.

Kufuor had been widely criticised by the media for his *globetrotting*. As head of the AU, his travel schedule was greatly intensified. In the first six months, he was estimated to have made 19 foreign trips. In mid-February, he attended the Franco-African summit in Cannes. He then flew to London for a state visit (12 March); to Senegal to attend the inauguration of President Wade (3 April); to South Africa to open the 7th ordinary session of the Pan-African parliament (4 May); to Libya (14 May); to Belgium to meet with the president of the EU (21 May) and then straight on to Ethiopia to deal with AU business, to Egypt and finally to Nigeria, where he attended the inauguration of President Yar'Adua. On 3 June, Kufuor flew to Switzerland and then on to Berlin to attend the G8 summit, before continuing to France to meet with President Sarkozy. On 14 June, he attended the summit of ECOWAS heads of state, at which the *ECOWAS Commission* was inaugurated with Dr. Ibn Chambas of Ghana as the first president. The second half of the year was slightly less gruelling. On 16 August, Kufuor travelled to Congo-Brazzaville and then on to Gabon. On 22 September, he was in New York to attend the 62nd session of the UN General Assembly. On 17 October, he flew to Equatorial Guinea to participate in the commissioning of a liquefied natural gas plant. On 23–25 November, he attended the Commonwealth heads of government meeting in Kampala. Finally, on 6 December Kufuor travelled to Portugal for the EU-Africa summit.

The AU presented Kufuor with many fresh responsibilities. On 16 February, he presided over the signing of an agreement among Sudan, Chad and the Central African Republic that was designed to promote good neighbourliness. On 4 February, President Laurent Gbagbo of Côte d'Ivoire visited Ghana for consultations. Then from 1–3 July, Ghana hosted the *AU summit* at which the main item on the agenda was movement in the direction of a Union government for Africa. Whereas Libya's leader Kadhafi was, as ever, in favour of more rapid progress, Kufuor sided with the pragmatist camp. The Accra Declaration of 3 July was a cautious document that focused on strengthening the regional economic communities as a first step towards eventual union.

Kufuor also received a number of official visits in his capacity as president of Ghana. On 11 January, German President Horst Köhler came with a business delegation and took part in an international conference on partnership.

Relations with China were further solidified. On 19 April, the countries signed six agreements that included the construction of the Bui dam and debt cancellation (including the costs of the construction of the national theatre). The Chinese delegation made it clear that the one-China policy, to which the Ghana government adhered, was central to this friendly arrangement.

The government continued to promote friendly relations with other *West African countries*. Kufuor was constantly supportive of Yar'Adua, despite the doubt that was cast over the Nigerian elections. On 11 January, the border with Côte d'Ivoire was briefly closed after an armed attack on the Ivorian border post of Noe, but relations between the governments were not affected. On 8 November, the newly installed president of Sierra Leone, Ernest Bain Koroma, paid a two-day state visit. Between 13 and 15 October, the Togolese authorities closed their side of the border during the period of the legislative elections. President Faure Gnassingbé visited on 16 November to engage in discussions about closer cooperation and was congratulated by Kufuor on his success in those polls. On 2 July, delegates from Ghana and Burkina Faso met to discuss joint management of the resources of the White Volta basin in the context of their ongoing cross-border cooperation plans. The only country with which relations were somewhat strained was Gambia. The murder of 44 Ghanaians in 2005, allegedly by Gambian security forces, remained a point of friction. Many blamed the government for not doing enough to get to the bottom of the affair. On 24 August, a delegation travelled to Banjul to investigate further, but the government refrained from accusing the Jammeh regime of complicity.

Ghana played an active role in the *UN* by virtue of its position as non-permanent member of the Security Council, which came to an end on 31 December. On 23 January, Kofi Annan returned to Ghana, having served out his second term as UN secretary general, and indicated his desire to retire in the country.

Socioeconomic Developments

On 8 February, President Kufuor gave his *state of the nation* address to parliament in which he expressed pride in the robust growth rate, relatively low inflation and falling interest rates. He placed particular emphasis on agriculture and the future role of science and technology in boosting production. The local chapter of Transparency International bemoaned the fact that there was no mention of anti-corruption measures. Bagbin launched a searing attack on the state of Ghana under the NPP, presenting it as a highly divided country in which corruption was rife, justice was partial, human rights abuses were legion and social inequalities were growing. He also criticised the over-hasty implementation of the National Health Insurance Scheme (NHIS).

In his address, President Kufuor also outlined initiatives to deal with the crippling *energy shortage*. He promised short-term relief from Nigeria and Côte d'Ivoire, but this failed to materialise because both the latter faced their own energy crises. In the long term, the government placed much of its hopes in an ECOWAS-wide scheme, which enjoyed the financial backing of the IDA, to expand generating capacity at Akosombo. The completion of the West African gas pipeline project, which would be used to supply thermal energy plants, was also eagerly awaited (the first gas flowed on 20 December), as was the completion of the Bui dam. These measures could only be welcomed by industry, which complained of the debilitating consequences of load shedding and unscheduled power cuts. On 15 March for example, the VALCO aluminium smelter was forced to close. Load shedding was suspended at the time of the anniversary celebrations in March to avoid embarrassment. However, the cuts resumed as soon as these ended. The NDC seized on the government's failure to deal with the problem. On 5 April, Atta-Mills issued a statement in which he pointed out that NDC strategic plans for energy had been shelved by the NPP. The CPP also reminded the NPP of the fact that Nkrumah had embarked on plans to increase energy supply, including construction of the Bui dam, but these were cancelled by the military junta and politicians of the Busia/Danquah tradition after he was overthrown. On 18 June, a British oil exploration company, Tullow Oil, announced that it had made a significant offshore *oil discovery*, and at exactly the same time an American company announced a similar find. This led to much rejoicing in the NPP. It was estimated that the country imported $ 1.1 bn worth of oil annually. On 22 December, President Kufuor estimated the oil reserves at three billion barrels.

On 1 July, the Bank of Ghana changed the *currency*, creating the New Ghana Cedi (¢). In effect, this took one zero off the old notes. The two versions of the cedi circulated alongside one another until the end of the year, with prices being quoted in both denominations. Despite predictions of confusion, the exercise passed off smoothly.

On 2 February, the vice president of the International Finance Corporation revealed that Ghana was ranked highest among the African countries and ninth overall in the IFC-World Bank doing business rankings for 2007. However, he identified persistent obstacles such as protracted and costly start-up times and lengthy import and export procedures. When the head of the World Bank, Paul Wolfowitz, visited on 2 March he similarly praised the success of the past ten years. On 20 June, the Ghana consultative group of donors promised to increase assistance from $ 1.2 bn to $ 1.4 bn per year for the next four years. On 2 February, parliament belatedly approved the *Millennium Challenge Account* agreement that unlocked $ 547 m of American funding for agricultural development. On 7 September, the European Commission agreed to support Ghana to the tune of ¢ 92.6 m, most of which consisted of budgetary support. As of April 2007, the total foreign debt of Ghana stood at $ 2.7 bn, of which $ 1.3 bn was owed to multilateral agencies. On 21 March, the governor of the Bank of Ghana, Paul Acquah, estimated that private remittances had brought in $ 5.78 bn in 2006.

On 15 November, the minister of finance and economic planning, Kwadwo Baah-Wiredu, presented his *budget*. He estimated economic growth for the year at 6.3% rather than the projected

6.5%, due to the energy crisis and erratic rainfall. The cocoa sector was badly affected by dry weather and it was anticipated that production would fall significantly at a time of rising world producer prices. However, the minister projected a real GDP growth rate of 7% in 2008. The budget deficit for 2007 was estimated at 4% of GDP. One of the more controversial measures was the decision to tax mobile phone airtime.

Textile manufacturing had been in decline for some years. On 1 July, a Chinese company reopened the Juapong textiles mill in partnership with the state. This was somewhat ironic, in that competition from cheap Chinese imports was partly what had precipitated its closure in 2005. In April, Ghana Telecom became 100% state-owned once again after Telekom Malaysia sold its 30% stake, following a rancorous relationship. Almost immediately, 51% of the shares of the company were put up for sale and were bought by France Telecom in November. In October, the government announced the sale of 75% of the shares in Western Telesystems, or Westel, to Celtel. The latter promised substantial new investments in the ailing *telecommunications* network.

On 27 April, the statistical service released the findings of the Ghana living standards survey, earlier versions of which had been conducted in 1991 and 1999. It found that the overall incidence of *poverty* had fallen from 51.7% in 1991 to 28.5% in 2005. This enabled the World Bank country director, Mats Karlsson, to suggest that Ghana was well on the way to meeting one of the key MDGs. The one major source of concern was that that the incidence of poverty in Greater Accra had increased, confirming more anecdotal evidence such as the increase in the number of street children. A World Bank survey released in early June noted a dramatic increase in urbanisation, which was considered partly to blame for the rising incidence of urban poverty. The 2007 United Nations Human Development Index placed Ghana 136th in the world, one place higher than the previous year. The report mentioned that half of the children in the north were malnourished compared with 13% in Accra, which rather confused the poverty profile.

On 20 January, the deputy minister of *health*, Samuel Owusu-Agyei, conceded that whereas the NHIS had achieved only 30% coverage in 2006, the target for 2007 was set at 55%. The backlog in identity cards was one particular problem that the authorities promised to address. Another was the debts that were owed to hospitals. The initiative received a boost when, on 3 July, the World Bank agreed to support the NHIS to the tune of $ 15 m. A further $ 25 m was allocated to nutrition and malaria control. In early February, former US President Jimmy Carter visited to check progress in the fight against guinea worm that was being partly funded by his trust. On 30 April, the head of the national AIDS control programme noted an increase in the HIV prevalence rate from 2.7% to 3.2%, with the Eastern Region recording the highest and the Northern Region the lowest rates of infection.

The issue of *employment* was bound to feature prominently in the year before an election. On 1 March, the Ghana investment promotion centre claimed that it had overseen the generation of 53,430 new jobs connected to 1,154 investments in projects. The national youth employment programme started late in 2006 and as of May claimed to have found work for 95,000 people. However, the initiative was dogged by claims of political partisanship.

The Ghana Education Trust (GET) fund was expected to disburse ¢ 582 bn (old) for the improvement of educational infrastructure in 2007, in addition to the ministerial allocation. However, there were allegations of misuse of the money following *student unrest* at the University of Ghana, whose management maintained that students could only be admitted into campus accommodation during their first year. The NDC accused the government of having used GET fund money to bankroll its youth employment scheme, which meant there was insufficient money to build new student accommodation.

The two interrelated social problems that came to the top of the political agenda were child labour and *child trafficking*, which caused Ghana a lot of adverse international publicity. Kufuor promised tougher action as Ghana slumped in the US State Department ratings for effective measures to deal with the trafficking problem. Over the course of the year, press reports of children being freed kept the issue in the public eye. It was suggested that many of the victims of internal trafficking came from the impoverished north and were despatched to fishing and cocoa farming areas as labourers or used as servants. Human trafficking was also kept in the public eye as Ghanaians commemorated the 200th anniversary of Britain's withdrawal from the slave trade. The British deputy prime minister, John Prescott, visited in February. He expressed regret for the slave trade and lamented the current incidence of human trafficking. Meanwhile, the NPP launched the Joseph Project (the name of which referred to the story of Joseph in Genesis) from 1 August, which was designed to reconnect African Americans with their African roots. However, Kufuor was widely criticised for distancing himself from the reparations movement.

In 2006, Ghana's reputation as an emerging transit point in the international *drugs trade* was highlighted in a number of cases. This included the arrest of the Nkoranza North MP and the Tagor/ Abass affair, implicating police officers, which culminated in convictions in November 2007. The case of two British teenagers of Ghanaian extraction who were arrested at Kotoka airport on 2 July in possession of a large quantity of cocaine attracted considerable international attention. The girls were found guilty. The US State Department singled out Ghana as a trans-shipment point for South American cocaine in its annual international narcotic control strategy report for 2007. On 9 February, Ghana signed agreements with the UN office on drugs and crime that were intended to bolster the capacity of the authorities to deal with drug smuggling and money laundering. The NPP promised legislation to deal specifically with the latter.

On 21 February, parliament passed a *domestic violence* bill that had been a source of controversy in the past. Women MPs of all parties regarded this as a victory. The debate about whether *homosexuality* should be legalised raged on and off during the year, with the government insisting that it had no intention of amending the law to accommodate practices it regarded as inherently un-Ghanaian. However, external pressure on the government was mounting and the issue was almost bound to provoke more debate in the future.

Ghana in 2008

Paul Nugent

The focal point of the year was the election of a new president and parliament. Although the polls were scheduled for December and in both cases won by the opposition National Democratic Congress (NDC), the greater part of 2008 was spent campaigning, given that the principal candidates had been selected at the end of 2007. Football briefly took centre stage in January when Ghana hosted the African Nations Cup, but failure to reach the finals meant that popular attention reverted to politics. In the first nine months, high oil prices and rising food prices squeezed consumers, but ironically the unfolding global economic crisis at the close of the year brought some relief.

Domestic Politics

In his New Year speech, President Kufuor noted that "Ghana's elections [had] become the benchmark for others on the continent" and promised that the government would do its part to ensure a repetition of this achievement. On 13 January, Nana Addo Dankwa Akufo-Addo of the New Patriotic Party (NPP) held a rally in Koforidua at which, flanked by 14 of the candidates who had contested the nomination, he indicated that the party was reunited following the controversy surrounding the congress in December 2007. However, a clear indication of *ongoing splits* came on 18 April when Alan Kyerematen announced his resignation, citing harassment of his supporters. Kufuor convened a meeting with Kyerematen and Akufo-Addo, following which the

 | DOI 10.1163/9789004308183_006

former rescinded his decision on 1 May. But the NDC was quick to point out that the affair cast doubt on NPP claims to be the paragon of democratic virtue, adding that Akufo-Addo had made similar complaints when he failed in his leadership bid against Kufuor in 1998. Another delicate matter was the selection of a *running mate*. There was active lobbying for a northern candidate, with the name of Boniface Saddique (MP for Salaga) being touted. On 14 August, Akufo-Addo decided on a party outsider, Dr. Mahamudu Bawumia. The youthful deputy governor of the Bank of Ghana lacked the baggage of some of the more established candidates.

Meanwhile, Kufuor was forced to deal with some rebelliousness in *government ranks*. On 11 January, he sacked his national security minister, Francis Poku, because of rumoured corruption and his inability to see eye to eye with service chiefs. A vigorous public debate ensued over whether or not Poku had been placed under house arrest. On 24 May, Kufuor dismissed Kwamena Bartels as minister of interior, replacing him with his brother, Dr. Kwame Addo-Kufuor.

The NDC encountered some difficulties of its own. The NPP press published rumours that party leader John Atta-Mills was very ill and therefore incapable of running the country. One NDC MP urged a rethink of the choice of candidate before being forced to retract. On 4 February, Mills issued a statement from South Africa stating that the *medical issue* was nothing more serious than treatment for cataracts and sinus problems. But doubts over his vigour made it imperative that Mills find a young, dynamic running mate who was preferably also a northerner. Despite Jerry and Nana Konadu Rawlings favouring Betty Mould-Iddrisu, and despite demands in Tamale that Alhaji Mumuni be re-selected, Mills eventually opted for John Mahama. The latter was a northern MP, but also a member of the Assemblies of God church. Although being a non-Muslim counted against him in some quarters, Mahama was quick to point out that his mother was Muslim.

Most commentators considered him an excellent choice and the disappointed candidates fell dutifully into line.

It was fortunate for the tenor of the subsequent campaign that Mahama and Bawumia considered each other friends, a relationship built on the close personal ties between their fathers. However, this did not prevent a certain amount of *mudslinging*. The pro-NDC press repeated allegations by the maverick politician, Kofi Wayo, that Akufo-Addo was addicted to hard drugs. This was damaging because it was known that the US was particularly concerned about Ghana as an emerging centre in the narcotics trade. On 4 February, Akufo-Addo's lawyers felt compelled to issue a statement denying that he had ever been apprehended in the US for being in possession of cocaine and denying categorically that he had a drugs problem.

On 22 February, the Electoral Commission (EC) removed a potential source of controversy when it announced that the diaspora vote, which had been fiercely opposed by the NDC, would not be operative in the coming elections. However, the accuracy of the *voters' register* remained a serious bone of contention. Before the reopening of the register, there were complaints that the figures for 13 Ashanti constituencies were massively inflated. On 11 April, the EC set up an independent committee to investigate. On 30 April, the EC chairman, Dr. Kwadwo Afari-Gyan, seemed to confirm the anomaly, although he cautioned against conspiracy theories. But on 10 June, he announced that the incorrect figures, which were the result of a printing error, only existed in hard copy and were not replicated in the EC's own database. On 14 March, the EC began the process of allowing those who had lost their voter ID cards to replace them. On 31 July, the limited voter registration exercise (11 days) began, to allow those who had reached the age of 18 to register. There were clashes in the north between NDC and NPP supporters over alleged attempts to register minors. The NDC also complained that there was a deliberate shortage of registration materials. The EC conceded that there had been unforeseen logistical problems and extended registration by a further two days. The credibility of the exercise was placed in doubt, however, when the EC revealed on 10 September that whereas it had been expecting up to one million new names, it had actually ended up with almost two million additions to the register. The tally of 12,822,474 registered voters was 16.7% higher than the figures for 2006, with the Upper East and Ashanti regions recording the highest percentage increases. Between 5 and 11 October, the register was exhibited at all polling stations in an effort to 'cleanse' it. The EC was able to excise 500,000 names, mostly a consequence of double-registration, which went some way towards allaying fears.

The choice of *parliamentary candidates* proved more of a problem for the NPP than the NDC. In Amansie-West, the incumbent MP was re-selected by a single vote on 11 May. When rival supporters demonstrated, the police cracked down in a heavy-handed manner. In many constituencies, aggrieved supporters of losing candidates threatened to vote 'skirt and blouse': that is, to vote for Akufo-Addo, but for a different parliamentary candidate. On 18 June, Kufuor, Akufo-Addo and NPP executives met to discuss the turmoil in the constituencies. However, any direct intervention was bound to prompt accusations of favouritism. On 14 March, a breakaway party, the Reformed Patriotic Democrats, was launched, and there were concerns that it would take crucial votes from the NPP. The creation of new districts and the choice of their capitals was also mired in controversy, and raised the possibility of a backlash.

The campaign was dominated by NDC and NPP allegations about each other's record in office. Akufo-Addo explicitly insisted that the two Kufuor administrations accomplished more than what was done during the entire 18-year period under

Rawlings. The NDC disputed the figures and alleged that the Kufuor regime had been wasteful and corrupt. The perception of declining *standards of probity* was one that harmed the NPP. The government did not help its cause by reappointing Dr. Richard Anane as minister for transportation in March after the case against him by the commission on human rights and administrative justice was overturned by the courts on a technicality in 2007. On 8 January, Kufuor thanked India for the completion of the new presidential palace, but the NDC maintained that it was actually a waste of Ghanaian public money. In March, a public row erupted over plans to buy a presidential jet. Minister of Defence Albert Kan Dapaah explained that each presidential visit to Europe cost Ghana about € 250,000 and that money would be saved. On 19 March, parliament also voted to approve a loan agreement for the purchase of two executive jets from China.

As in previous elections, the *smaller parties* struggled to find a public voice. On 30 January, Dr. Edward Mahama of the People's National Convention appeared to welcome an alliance with the NDC. This was followed by a rumour in May that Mahama was willing to team up with the Convention People's Party (CPP) as the running mate to Dr. Paa Kwesi Nduom. Mahama was slow to respond, but on 22 May he rejected such an alliance blaming Nduom for having gone public before an agreement had been sealed. Mahama became the only candidate to field a female running mate, Petra Amegashie. Meanwhile, Nduom, who chose a northern running mate, sought to inject renewed vigour into the CPP. However, the veteran MP for Ellembelle, Freddie Blay, endorsed Akufo-Addo. Nduom supporters demanded his expulsion, but the reality was that Nduom had done precisely the same thing to the CPP candidate in 2004. On 9 October, a fast track court ruled against the party's attempts to disqualify Blay as a parliamentary candidate.

As his term wound down, the *president* sought to remove possible excuses for an NDC administration to seek revenge. On 25 May, he pardoned Dan Abodakpi, who had been jailed in 2007 for causing financial loss to the state. But any goodwill evaporated when Tsatsu Tsikata, the former head of the Ghana National Petroleum Corporation (GNPC), was sentenced to an 18-year term of imprisonment. Kufuor surprised everyone when he announced on 24 May that he was conferring a national honour on Mills. After some delay, Mills turned the offer down. Kufuor compounded the embarrassment by honouring himself with a new award, complete with a solid gold medal.

On 14 March, the coalition of domestic election observers despatched its first local observers nine months in advance of the polls. Meanwhile, the NDC and the NPP trained a total of 270,000 polling agents between them, covering all of the 22,000 polling stations in the 230 constituencies. On 5 May, nine political parties signed up to a joint communiqué committing themselves to free and peaceful elections. However, as the campaign heated up, there were a number of incidents. On 2 June, a man was killed as he entered the compound of the Volta regional minister, Kofi Dzamesi, with the alleged intention of assassinating him. Dzamesi claimed it was part of a plot to destabilise the region. On 31 August and 1 September, there were fatal clashes between NPP and NDC supporters in Tamale, where Bawumia's convoy was attacked, and in Gushiegu, prompting concern amongst *election observers*. On 21 September, there were further clashes at Berekum in Brong-Ahafo. The greatest potential powder keg was Bawku in the Upper East, where there was sporadic ethnic *violence* between Mamprusis and Kusasis. On 1 January, Interior Minister Bartels declared a curfew after fighting that led to numerous deaths, and this was renewed right through the elections. On 4 May and on 22 June, there were renewed outbreaks of violence and a significant number of mortalities. MPs from the north complained that

Kufuor had done little to mediate in Bawku, whereas he was active in conflict situations abroad.

In the closing stages of the campaign, the candidates toured the regions. Akufo-Addo made a special appeal to northern voters, promising a $ 1 bn northern development fund. Kufuor announced on 11 September that a draft bill would be expedited to make this a reality. The NDC responded with *campaign promises* to create a savannah development fund. In the south, Akufo-Addo promised a pension scheme for cocoa farmers. Everywhere, Akufo-Addo pledged an increased level of public spending, especially on health and education. He promised a university and factory for every region, which the NDC derided as reckless. Rawlings popped up repeatedly on the NDC campaign trail, attacking corruption and alleging NPP intentions to rig. On 17 September, the national security council announced a ban on seven former service commanders from entering all military and police installations "in the interests of national security" after they had met with Rawlings.

On 2 December, service personnel with election duties cast their special ballots. The main poll followed on 7 December. The *parliamentary results* were a blow to the NPP, whose representation fell from 128 to 107 seats, whereas the NDC increased its tally from 94 to 114 seats and won a majority in seven of the ten regions. With two constituencies needing to be re-run, the NDC was well placed to command an overall majority. Among the shock defeats were those of Blay (CPP) and Saddique (NPP). Samia Nkrumah, the daughter of Kwame Nkrumah, won the only seat for the CPP. In the presidential race, Akufo-Addo topped the poll, but because he only gained 49.13% there needed to be a *presidential run-off* on 28 December. Nduom (1.34%), Mahama (0.87%) and four other candidates were eliminated. In the run-off, there was a swing to Mills, but the EC chairman, Afari-Gyan, accepted that the Tain constituency, where there had been no polling, would have to vote because there was a statistical possibility of Akufo-Addo winning. Bizarrely, the NPP boycotted, making the final result a foregone conclusion. The EC figures revealed Mills had secured eight regions and 50.23% of the vote. Although the successful outcome was lauded by the international community, the official turnout in a number of constituencies in Ashanti stretched credibility.

Foreign Affairs

Kufuor maintained a punishing schedule of foreign visits. The year began with the post-election crisis in *Kenya*, in which Kufuor, in his capacity as chairman of the AU, sought to mediate. Some embarrassment was caused when the Kenyan incumbents indicated that his services were not needed. On 8 January, Kufuor arrived at the invitation of Mwai Kibaki, but the authorities insisted that this was merely a fact-finding mission. When Kufuor departed two days later, he explained that his intention had been to encourage Kibaki and Raila Odinga to agree to a cessation of hostilities and to engage in dialogue under the aegis of a group of eminent Africans. He announced that Kofi Annan had accepted the assignment of leading a team.

Kufuor continued to invest time in *ECOWAS*. On 18 January, he flew to Ouagadougou to attend an ECOWAS summit of heads of state. On 27 February, he received a joint UN/ECOWAS mission to discuss ways of bringing stability to the north of Mali, Niger and Mauritania where rebel activity posed renewed problems. On 19 December, Kufuor attended the 35th ordinary session of ECOWAS heads of state in Abuja, his last as president.

On 28 January, Kufuor travelled to Addis Ababa for the 10th ordinary session of the AU, at which a new chairman was elected, taking over from the Ghanaian president. From there, Kufuor continued to Rome to attend the annual general meeting of the WFP. On 12 March, he visited Nigeria for talks with President Umaru Yar'Adua, and then on 19 March he flew to Paris for the launch of The Alliance for Africa Foundation. On 3 April, he passed through London to attend a progressive governance summit, and then continued to India to participate in the first *Africa-India summit*. Kufuor stated that African countries had much to learn from India, especially with respect to information and communication technologies. On 4 May, Kufuor travelled back to London to attend a conference on private/public sector partnership in attaining MDGs. On 24 May, he flew to Japan for the Tokyo international conference on African development and then on to the World Economic Forum in Cape Town. Between 30 June and 1 July, Kufuor attended the 11th ordinary session of the AU Assembly in Egypt. On 5 July, he left once more for Japan to attend the G8 summit, which began with a day devoted to Africa. At the start of August, Kufuor spent a further two weeks abroad, first visiting Trinidad and Tobago before proceeding to the opening of the Olympic games in Beijing.

As his term of office wound down, Kufuor received *many official invitations*. On 25 August, he paid a three-day state visit to Germany, where he was awarded the highest state honour. Between 21 and 24 October, Kufuor was the guest of the Netherlands. His next stop was London, where he received the Chatham House prize in a ceremony presided over by the Duke of Edinburgh for his contribution to conflict mediation. President George W. Bush went further than anyone to acknowledge the role played by Kufuor. On 19 February, Bush arrived in Ghana as part of a five-country African tour. The visit prompted opposition speculation that the Americans were seeking a military base, but this was vigorously denied by Foreign Minister Akwasi

Osei-Adjei. Much of the attention during the visit was focused on development cooperation, with Bush announcing a $ 350 m fund to fight neglected tropical diseases. Laura Bush launched a malaria initiative for Ghana worth $ 17 m. In 2008, an estimated $ 75 m was to be spent in 23 districts on education, water, sanitation and electrification with money derived from the Millennium Challenge Account. On 11 September, President Bush returned the favour when Kufuor was invited to Washington for a farewell *state visit* that included a lavish banquet at the White House. Kufuor was praised for his international contribution and record as two-term president. From Washington, Kufuor continued to New York, where he used his final appearance at the UN General Assembly to highlight the achievements under his stewardship and to renew Ghana's commitment to the MDGs.

Ghana hosted three *major international conferences*. Between 18 and 25 April, it hosted a meeting of UNCTAD on the opportunities and challenges presented by globalisation. Escalating world food prices were a key item on the agenda. The meeting was attended by UN Secretary General Ban Ki-moon, President Bai Koroma of Sierra Leone and President Lula da Silva of Brazil, who also used the occasion to sign four bilateral agreements covering energy, health, biodiversity and HIV/AIDS. From 2–4 September, Ghana hosted the Third High Level Forum on Aid Effectivenes (HLF3), which was attended by a number of heads of state and closed by Kufuor. International and Ghanaian NGOs were critical of the lack of substance in the Accra agenda for action that promised greater harmonisation of effort and ownership by recipient countries. Between 30 September and 3 October, Ghana hosted the 6th biennial summit of the ACP countries. The summit was as controversial as HLF3, because the EU was seeking reciprocal trade concessions with ACP countries through EPAs. Ghana had already signed interim EPAS, whereas other West African states regarded the latter as the thin end of the wedge. President Omar al-Bashir of Sudan, who had been indicted by the ICC in July, made his scheduled speech, which condemned the ICC action, and departed early. The meeting requested the ICC to suspend the indictment.

Kufuor also engaged in some *bilateral diplomacy*. On 4 February, President Teodoro Obiam Mbasogo of Equatorial Guinea visited to discuss cooperation in the oil sector. On 17 February, President Levy Mwanawasa of Zambia stopped in Accra en route to Gambia. On 2 September, following Mwanawasa's sudden death, Kufuor attended the funeral. Between 17 and 19 April, Malian President Amadou Toumane Toure paid a state visit during which he was hosted by the Asantehene and awarded the country's highest state honour. In the first week of November, the president of Trinidad and Tobago, George Richards, paid a return state visit to Ghana. On 22 November, Kufuor travelled to Liberia for a two-day official visit.

In 2007, goods worth an estimated $ 200 m were imported from China, while statistics from the Ghana investment promotion centre indicated that *China* had become the largest foreign investor. On 18 January, a Chinese chamber of commerce meeting opened in Accra. On 18 April, Kufuor inaugurated work on the 560 MW Sunon Asogli Kpone thermal power plant, a private sector initiative involving the Shenzen Energy Group and the China-Africa Development Fund. The paramount chief of Asogli, Togbe Afede XIV, was credited with having brought the idea to fruition. The inauguration provided an occasion for Shenzen businessmen to visit. At the end of May, the first phase in the creation of a fibre optic network to sustain broadband connectivity, which was financed with a Chinese concessionary loan, was completed. On 2 September, an agreement was signed with the Sino Hydro Corporation for the construction of four dams in the western and central regions that were expected to generate 230 MW of electricity within three years. On 4 December, a new Chinese-built complex for the ministry of defence was commissioned.

Socioeconomic Developments

On 14 February, President Kufour delivered his final *state of the nation* address. This provided him with the occasion to document the achievements since 2001. In the educational sector, he claimed that the Ghana school feeding programme had been held up as a model for developing countries, while he highlighted disease prevention as the cornerstone of health policy. He proudly announced that Ghana had launched a Euro-Bond on the London Stock Exchange to raise $ 750 m for infrastructural development and to withstand the shocks associated with rising oil prices. He also noted the successful redenomination of the cedi, which was completed in the first days of January. Kufuor looked to oil to remove important structural constraints on development and reduce donor dependency. The NDC observed that action against corruption did not receive much emphasis, which was surprising given the potential for oil revenues to introduce unprecedented temptations. However, on 22 February Kufuor formally acknowledged the need for mechanisms to ensure accountability and transparency in the use of oil revenues.

The first half of the year was dominated by soaring prices for imported petroleum and foodstuffs. On 28 January, Dr. Paul Acquah, governor of the central bank, announced that *inflation* had risen to 12.7%, in December. By July, it had peaked at 18.4%, but it fell back to 17.3% in October as food prices began to recede. Acquah also stated that the public debt of $ 7.1 bn had fallen from 50.9% of GDP in 2006 to 48.4% in 2007. On 28 October, Acquah noted that the crisis in the global financial markets and the subsequent contraction of the global economy had not had an immediate effect on Ghana. Indeed, the first half of the year witnessed a seven-fold increase in *foreign direct investment*, led by China and India. On 19 May, the government signed a second multi-donor budget support framework memorandum, revising an agreement signed in 2003. The total disbursement in budgetary support was expected to be $ 350 m over the course of the year. The conference on aid effectiveness (HLF3) provided the occasion for Ghana and the British government to sign a £ 250 m aid agreement covering 2008–10, mostly for budgetary support. At the same time, Ghana signed two agreements with Switzerland, worth $ 13 m, and an agreement with the EU to curb illegal timber exports.

In order to alleviate some of the pressure on consumers, the government reduced *excise duties* on petroleum products on 22 May. It followed up on 13 June with the removal of duties on imported rice, yellow maize and vegetables. The customs, excise and preventive service observed that the net effect would be a significant revenue shortfall. On 14 July, the government announced the reintroduction of subsidies on fertilisers. The poorer parts of the country were considered to be severely affected and WFP allocated $ 3.4 m to supporting families in the three northern regions.

In his New Year's speech, Kufuor confirmed that the West African gas pipeline project was complete. On 3 January, a nuclear power committee reported its findings on how to provide a nuclear energy alternative by 2018. On 18 April, Akufo-Addo lent guarded support to the idea in a statement on energy. GNPC expected that *oil production* capacity towards the end of 2009 would be 60,000 bpd. The two main exploration companies, Tullow and Kosmos Energy, were confident that output would be double that by 2010 after announcing further promising finds. On 26 February, a Norwegian delegation promised to make its expertise available to Ghana. On 3 June, a Russian oil company, Lukoil, indicated that it would begin onshore oil exploration in the second half of the year.

On 20 June, the government bought the remaining 10% of shares in the Volta Aluminium Company (VALCO). On 7 November, parliament ratified the re-sale of 70% of the shares, as part of a plan to create an integrated *aluminium* industry. However, it turned out that the Brazilian and Norwegian investors were lukewarm about the acquisition. On 22 September, the government announced it was cancelling debts of $ 58 m owed by the Volta River Authority (VRA), the Electricity Company of Ghana and the Ghana Water Company Limited. The VRA was also one of the beneficiaries of the Eurobond issue.

The *gold* sector performed well in the first half of the year, due to a combination of higher prices and an expansion of output by 3%. By contrast, earnings from the diamond mining sector contracted by 22% over the same period. Tourism was the fourth largest foreign exchange earner in 2008. Having grown by 13% since 2007, it was worth $ 1.3 bn.

On 28 January, Cadbury announced the creation of a development fund to help improve *cocoa* yields and raise the income of farmers. On 29 January, the ministry of finance and the cocoa board signed a memorandum of understanding with 32 contractors vested with responsibility for completion of the first phase of the cocoa roads implementation project. This would improve 205 km of roads in the cocoa-producing regions. On 5 September, the government announced an early start to the cocoa season and increased the producer price by 36% in an attempt to reduce smuggling. The minister of finance, Kwadwo Baah-Wiredu, estimated that at least 50,000 tonnes had been smuggled, mostly to Côte d'Ivoire, that year. The minister also announced that the cocoa board would operate a stabilisation fund to hedge against price swings. On 1 October, Kufuor announced that Ghana expected to be able to process around half of the annual crop locally by the middle of 2010.

Mobile phone coverage was expected to reach 50% by 2010. On 3 January, the government indicated that it had reopened the search for a majority stakeholder for *Ghana Telecom*, having rejected the existing bids. At the end of June, news leaked that the government planned to sell 70% of its stake to Vodafone UK. The sale was opposed by the NDC and the CPP. Although the enabling legislation failed to pass before the recess on 19 July, parliament was recalled and it was approved on 14 August. However, the government was forced to issue a bond to cover the outstanding debts.

At the start of 2008, the doctor to patient ratio stood at 1:9,090 and the nurse to patient ratio at 1:1,538. On 7 March, Minister of Health Courage Quashigah announced that each new district capital would receive its own hospital. The keystone of government *health policy* remained the national health insurance scheme that was partly financed by a 2.5% levy on goods and services and partly by subscriptions. Whereas government aimed at covering 30% of the population by 2010, on 20 April officials estimated that coverage was already around 48%. Despite presidential praise for the school feeding programme, the chairman was sacked on 24 April following opposition allegations of misuse of funds and concerns expressed by the auditors.

The *University* of Ghana marked its 60th anniversary, with the celebrations reaching their climax in July. On 2 October, the University of Cape Coast made Ghanaian history when it appointed the first woman vice chancellor in the shape of Naana Opoku-Agyeman.

Ghana's reputation for adherence to international norms was somewhat tarnished after the deportation of 16 Liberian *refugees* following a sit-in demonstration at Buduburam camp on 19 February. The deportations were publicly criticised by UNHCR, but Minister of the Interior Bartels insisted that circumstances in

Liberia no longer posed an obstacle to return and that the refugees had refused to integrate. Some 500 Togolese were repatriated from the Volta region in March and April with the cooperation of UNHCR.

On 24 January, Bartels admitted in parliament that Ghana had become a significant node in the *drugs trade*. He also accepted that there had been some infiltration of the security agencies by narcotics interests. On 16 June, an official of the United Nations Office on Drugs and Crime (UNODC) visited to discuss modalities for a pilot scheme to monitor shipping containers at Tema harbour. Three days later, Dr. Addo-Kufuor met officials of the US Drugs Enforcement Agency (DEA) and highlighted Ghanaian initiatives, including the introduction of new X-ray facilities at Kotoka airport and the introduction of coastal speedboat patrols. On 22 October, President Kufuor announced that the DEA would open an office in Ghana.

Ghana in 2009

Michael Amoah

The year ushered in the administration of the National Democratic Congress (NDC), previously in opposition, following a tightly fought election that saw the exit of the incumbent National Patriotic Party (NPP) after eight years in power. The new government met a challenging fiscal balance and had recourse to the IMF, but vowed to bring transparency and accountability to oil dealings. Oil appeared to be a resource from which all political programmes could be supported, having whetted local and international appetites alike. In line with its aim to fulfil campaign promises, the government sought to justify the continuation of existing projects and, among other things, got to grips with the delicate and politicised task of handling conflicts in the northern part of the country. US President Barack Obama visited Ghana on his Africa foreign policy trip.

Domestic Politics

The December 2008 presidential and parliamentary elections were completed on 2 January after a run-off. The new president, John Atta Mills, defeated his opponent by a mere 40,586 votes nationally, in an election that was certified by observers as the freest and fairest to date in Africa, prompting the international community to praise the country's democratisation process, and earning Ghana the privilege of being chosen as the venue for US President Obama's first official visit to Africa. Attention soon turned to how domestic politics would pan out, particularly in

 | DOI 10.1163/9789004308183_007

key areas of electoral concern, such as jobs and the economy. Hence the budget, *appointments* and justice became three testing areas. Signs that the new administration was not a government-in-waiting began to show in difficulties with both national and international appointments. Diplomatic appointments were not finalised until as late as August.

In the interim, the government's attempt to redress the status quo was naturally viewed as the politics of vengeance, and this, rather than national priorities and real government business, appeared to take centre stage in popular perceptions during the first half of the year. In particular, there was turmoil about the purported ex-gratia *emoluments* for the former president, which constituted a long list including two houses, six cars, 60 days of overseas travel each year, and over $ 1 m in annual expenses. President Mills suspended disbursement of the emoluments and, in March, appointed a committee on emoluments chaired by Ishmael Yamson to review the basis for the entitlements determined by the previous presidential committee on emoluments chaired by Mrs Chinery-Hesse. In July, the Ishmael Yamson committee concluded that it could not establish the authorship of the two unsigned final reports of the Chinery-Hesse committee, and furthermore could not determine which of the unsigned reports was approved by the ex-president and parliament.

The new government pledged to fight corruption and prosecute the previous administration's corrupt officials. The attorney general was tasked to prepare a list, to which directive the NPP replied that they were not intimidated. The Ghanaian obsession with cars became a huge problem for the government to handle. On 9 January, the government ordered a return of all *state vehicles* in the possession of former ministers and government appointees, and suspended with immediate effect the re-registration of such vehicles with the drivers and vehicle licensing authority. The government also demanded a list of all state vehicles transferred into private ownership since June 2008, and directed that any further transfers be subject to the approval of the chief director at the office of the presidency.

All *security operatives* of the previous administration from 2001 to 2008 in the intelligence services, police, army and foreign service were laid off by the new security bosses. In a tit for tat measure for what occurred when the NPP took office in 2001, political appointees were instated across sectors where applicable, seeing to the exit of the appointees of the previous administration.

A series of *corruption* revelations about the NPP administration began to surface, especially the sale of Ghana Telecom to Vodafone UK, and the acquisition of the Kosmos Energy stake in the Jubilee Oil Field. Both revelations directly implicated the former president and his cronies. However, the new government's zealous anti-corruption campaign received a setback when, on 25 June, the sports minister, Mohammed Muntaka Mubarak, resigned over allegations of corruption and was replaced in a government reshuffle with Akua Sena Dansua, who was the minister for women and children's affairs. Furthermore, in September, a British Serious Fraud Office investigation indicted Dr Sipa Yankey, the minister of health, and Amadi Seidu, a minister of state at the presidency, over allegations of taking bribes from the British construction company Mabey & Johnson. The two ministers resigned on 9 October, even though the transactions in question occurred in 1996, when they were both serving in different capacities under an NDC government. The British court that handled the case ordered Mabey & Johnson to pay a package including reparations of £ 658,000 to the Ghanaian government.

Despite the change in government and signs of uncertainty in some quarters, the *central bank* enjoyed stability and integrity under the firm hand of its experienced governor Dr Paul Acquah, who had won the Banker of the Year – Africa award in 2008. He retired in September. But the position of his *deputy* Dr Mahamudu Bawumia became immediately untenable after the elections, since he had stood as vice-presidential candidate on an NPP ticket. He resigned in January and took up appointments first, in May, as visiting professor at the University of British Columbia, and subsequently, in November, as a senior associate member of St Antony's College and visiting senior research associate at the Centre for the Study of African Economies at the University of Oxford.

High among the government's challenges were uncompleted national projects, empty coffers and a huge budget deficit of 14.9%. Hence, the 2009 *budget* attracted extensive debate, including whether it could be the effective instrument for delivering on the key electoral promise of creating jobs, or at least engineering their creation in the medium and long term. The government got locked in protracted talks with civil servants over salary increases, arrears and the implementation of the new single spine salary structure. These funds were later allocated in the 2010 budget, announced on 19 November.

The government inherited an existing proposal to divide the *Northern Region* into two administrative regions. On 28 October, Vice President John Mahama received presentations in Accra from a delegation of the Northern Regional House of Chiefs, and decided to set up a technical committee that would prepare the case for carving up the region, in accordance with provisions in the Constitution. While it did not intend to cultivate a special focus on the underdeveloped north, the new administration found itself grappling with *conflicts* in this area, particularly in Bawku and Dagbon. A string of curfews was imposed on the Bawku municipality and environs because of renewed clashes in the longstanding conflict between Kusasis and Mamprusis.

In Dagbon, both the Andani Gate and the rival Abudu Gate also made their impressions. On 16 January, the Andani Gate officially commenced lobbying to reopen the case of the murder in 2002 of the former regent of Dagbon, Ya-Na Yakubu Andani, alleging that the Wuako commission of the previous NPP government had failed to identify the culprits. The Andanis had voted massively for the NDC in the December 2008 elections. The president promised, in his 20 February state of the nation address, to bring justice to the resolution of these armed crises. Amidst the complexity of the security situation, the vice president warned, in a speech on 7 March in Tamale, that the ban on possession of weapons would be enforced irrespective of political, ethnic or other affiliation.

The conflicts already had a history of *politicisation*. At a news conference in Tamale on 20 May, the Abudu Gate called on the president to remove the Northern Regional minister, Stephen Nayina, from office on the allegation that he was interfering in the Dagbon chieftaincy dispute and not abiding by the roadmap to peace as drawn up by the committee of eminent chiefs. Furthermore, as chair of the Northern Regional Security Council, he had provided security for an elder of the Andani Gate to renovate a sacred room in the Gbewaa Palace. The nature of the political minefield prompted Mills to state, in a speech during an official visit to Wa on 30 May, that the government would not interfere in chieftaincy issues. The Alliance for Accountable Governance had warned the president to proceed cautiously and with circumspection on the Dagbon case, which featured in his state of the nation address. In parliament, on 15 September, the NPP called for the minister of interior and national security, Cletus Avoka, to be reassigned because he was a Kusasi and too attached to the Bawku conflict to implement an impartial solution. The president summarily assured citizens, in a Yendi speech on 6 December, that the government was working seriously behind the scenes to bring justice to the Dagbon and Gusghiegu crises. Gushiegu is among townships on which curfews were imposed during the year.

Foreign Affairs

The highlight of Ghana's foreign affairs was *President Obama*'s visit to Accra on 10 July. Ongoing areas of cooperation with the US included projects under the Millennium Challenge Account and military exercises with the US Africa Command in relation to maritime security for the oil industry and drugs trafficking. The Ghanaian online media reported on 16 September that Ghana had placed orders for four air force planes and other defence equipment worth $ 680 m from the US Defense Security Cooperation Agency. Obama used his speech in Accra to outline US foreign policy on Africa.

There were no dramatic foreign policy shifts. The new government continued with Ghana's *longstanding policy* of maintaining itself in good standing with its neighbours, pursuing Pan-Africanism passionately, interacting positively with all well-meaning international partners, and in the process remaining unaligned to any superpower, while recognising international law and the centrality of the UN in global governance.

The controversial *appointment* of the inexperienced Alhaji Mohammed Mumuni as foreign minister made headlines, and the government took too long over the appointment of representatives to the biggest missions abroad – an ambassador to the US and a high commissioner to the UK – both of which took effect in September. President Mills made an official visit to the UK from 4 to 9 May before appointing Danso Boafo as high commissioner. The offices of the ministry of foreign affairs caught fire on 21 October, forcing the department to relocate temporarily. The

Chinese government offered to construct a new office complex, to be situated close to the Accra airport junction.

On 25 March, the vice president held wide-ranging trade and political discussions in Ouagadougou with President Blaise Compaoré of Burkina Faso, during which Compaoré called for the resumption of the Joint Commission for Cooperation to take forward a number of projects, including the proposed rail link between Ouagadougou and Kumasi which would facilitate trade between the two countries. The sensitive issue of the rise of water levels at the Bagre Dam in Burkina Faso, which leads to flooding in northern Ghana, was included in the discussions. When the Bagre Dam was opened on 4 September, it took just two days to flood the White Volta in northern Ghana and its tributaries, and prompted the rapid response team of Ghana's National Disaster Management Organisation, and a team from the 48th Engineer Regiment of the Ghana Army, to attend to the situation on 8 September.

In response to Mills' visit to Côte d'Ivoire in April, his Ivorian counterpart President Laurent Gbagbo met with him in Accra on 4 November, when both leaders agreed to reactivate the Ghana-Côte d'Ivoire Permanent Joint Commission for Cooperation, and Mills pledged Ghanaian assistance towards a peaceful presidential election in Côte d'Ivoire. One issue in Ghanaian-Ivorian cooperation has been the problem of cocoa smuggling. A more sensitive problem concerned demarcation of the common sea border, because of recent oil prospecting in this part of the Gulf of Guinea. This was in tandem with the agreement at the 13–14 February ECOWAS ministerial meeting to define national ocean and sea boundaries in accordance with the UN Convention on the Law of the Sea, and Ghana's own procedures with the UN Commission on the Limits of the Continental Shelf for an extension beyond the mandatory 200 nautical miles. On 6 November, the Ivorian government donated $ 60,000 to Ghana's future foreign office complex.

Relations with Togo resumed normality at various levels. On 19 June, the Ghana Water Company announced the launch of the Sogakope-Lomé Water Project with the Togo Water Company for the construction and operation of a water treatment plant and pipeline that would transport water from the Volta River to Lomé. The Togolese authorities aired their displeasure about Ghana permitting opposition leader Gilchrist Olympio to interact with President Obama during his visit to Accra. However, at a meeting in Accra on 26 August, Mills and his Togolese counterpart agreed to reconvene the Joint Border Demarcation Commission, which would facilitate the implementation of the ECOWAS protocol on the free movement of people, goods and services.

On 19 June, Mills visited Nigeria. A deal brokered to increase Nigerian oil supplies from 45,000 to 60,000 barrels a day could not be implemented. There was general concern about the influx of Nigerians and crime levels in Ghana. The Nigerian high commissioner to Ghana announced on 9 July that 300 Nigerians were serving jail terms in Ghanaian prisons. From 23 November to 2 December, Ghanaian naval security intercepted and returned a Nigerian oil vessel, which had been hijacked by pirates in the Gulf of Guinea.

EU aid included a € 175 m MDG contract facility, approved on 2 July. Ghana also hosted several *meetings*. From 24–25 August, the ECOWAS Small Arms Programme conference took place to identify armed violence reduction projects. Subsequently, on 2 September, the Ghanaian authorities agreed to ratify the ECOWAS Convention on Small Arms and Light Weapons and the Convention on Cluster Munitions. From 16 to 21 November, the First Pan-Africa Trade Fair and Investment Conference took place in Accra. From 23 to 27 November, the International African Coffee Organisation held its annual General Assembly in the Ghanaian capital, coinciding with the Eighth General Meeting of the African Coffee Research Network. From 7 to 8 December, Accra was the venue for the All Africa Energy Summit.

Socioeconomic Developments

A Comprehensive Food Security and Vulnerability Analysis (CFSVA), launched by the UN's World Food Programme in Accra on 6 May, outlined that 1.2 million people were insecure, with limited access to sufficient and nutritious *food*. Some 0.5 million in the rural areas of the three northern regions were determined to be at risk, while up to 1.5 million in the remaining seven regions faced comparable problems. The CFSVA cited the Upper West Region as the most affected area, where 34% of the population were food insecure, followed by the Upper East Region with 15%, and the Northern Region with 10%. The main causes of food insecurity included reliance on traditional and often inefficient agricultural practices, limited markets for farm produce, high food prices, lack of education and hazards such as weather conditions. On 13 November, two state-of-the-art laboratories sponsored by the Swiss government through the UN Industrial Development Organisation's Trade Capacity Building Project were opened at the Ghana Standards Board, to be used to test Ghana's agricultural exports. The accredited laboratories would assist Ghanaian exporters to ensure food safety, detect pesticide residues and reduce costs of testing, in order to boost consumer confidence in Ghanaian export products.

The new administration resolved to restructure the beleaguered National *Health* Insurance Scheme. The government responded to the demands of doctors for higher salaries, instituted the decentralisation of administrative processes that compelled health workers to travel to the capital, and promised to upgrade existing health training institutions or establish new ones. On 6 August, the Upper East Region director of health services, Dr Awoonor-Williams, expressed concern that none of the 57 newly qualified medical doctors nationwide chose postings to the region, adding that the doctor to patient ratio was 1:34,000. UNICEF also raised concerns about maternal deaths in the Upper West Region. According to the Zabzugu/Tatale District director of health, UNICEF and the Danish International Development Agency donated 16,000 insecticide-treated mosquito nets for free distribution to motivate pregnant women to attend district health facilities for delivery. The results of a survey conducted in six communities of the Birim Central Municipality and the Birim South District revealed that about 10% of teenagers between the ages of 11 and 14 were sexually active, either because of the influence of sex videos or driven by hardship. In the course of the year, the National Health Insurance Authority suspended two private hospitals in Kumasi for faulty prescriptions and over-billing.

The government signed an agreement with the Ghana National Association of Teachers for a 17% salary increment for teachers (as reported in July), while awaiting implementation of another salary structure early in the next year. On 3 August, it announced cabinet approval for senior high school reforms, reducing *education* by one year. On 24 August, the government announced an increase in grants for school meals, while it also began implementing distribution of free school uniforms to poorer pupils. On 19 November, the government announced an initiative to provide permanent buildings for schools currently operating under trees, and to expand facilities in schools still running on a shift system. The 19 November budget statement made provision for constructing and furnishing 165 school buildings to accommodate primary and junior high schools, and 250 structures for kindergartens, in the next three years.

The GDP *growth* rate for 2008 was over 7%, but being cognisant of the global credit crunch and the decline in remittances, plus an inherited budget deficit of 14.9%, the new government proposed a modest and realistic target of 5.9% growth in 2009. This was the first time in nine years that the annual growth rate of GDP was expected to fall below the level for the previous year. Inflation had skyrocketed from 18.1% in December 2008 to 20.5% in March 2009, and to 20.7% in June. With the budget deficit and financial difficulties ahead, the government went to the IMF and obtained a three-year $ 1.2 bn interest-free package to support the budget, in addition to World Bank support. The package came with conditions and other triggers, such as a jobs freeze in the public sector, except for teachers, nurses and doctors, for at least two years, and a halt to subsidising petrol prices – both measures that were in sharp contrast with campaign promises. Experts viewed the move as a setback for the country's development and a reminder of similar IMF conditions for structural adjustment during the 1980s and 1990s under the previous NDC administration, which had failed to work. The NPP administration had worked very hard to wean the country from such arrangements by raising sovereign bonds from the international capital market. The government, however, achieved 4.7% GDP growth for 2009 and set a more aspirational 6.5% GDP target for the next year. *Inflation* was reduced to 17% at the end of the year, on the basis of which the government set a 14.5% target for 2010. The reduction in inflation, coupled with a sharp decline in the depreciation of the cedi against the US dollar from 5.4% in January to 0.9% in July, and a subsequent steady appreciation of the cedi from July, became the first real signs of macroeconomic stability. In December, the cedi appreciated by 0.2% against the US dollar, 1% against the British pound, 1% against the euro, and 1% against the South African rand.

Gold exports for the first half of the year increased by 1.2%, from $ 1,199 m in 2008 to $ 1,213 m, but diamond exports declined significantly from $ 29.5 m in 2008 to $ 3.1 m. Exports of *cocoa* and related products for the first half of the year amounted to $ 1,060 m, an annual growth of 16.6% compared with $ 910 m in 2008. The cocoa harvest for the full season of 2008/09 was 703,000 tonnes, up by 3% from the preceding year's figure of 680,000 tonnes. In September, the price of cocoa rose on the London international market to its highest since 1989 and, in response, the government increased the producer price with effect from 14 October. On 3 September, the Ghana Cocoa Board announced that the crop year bonuses from the last season had been released to the Licence Buying Companies for payment to all cocoa farmers. On 3 November, Cadbury Ghana and Cadbury Canada donated 5,000 bicycles to be distributed to school children in deprived cocoa growing communities to increase access to education.

In order to ensure more efficient revenue administration, the president, himself a *tax* expert, welcomed representations from the Chartered Institute of Taxation on 10 September. Subsequently, on 19 November, the government announced that the three revenue collection agencies would be amalgamated under a single commissioner general. New software was also introduced to facilitate the prompt preparation and submission of tax returns.

On 7 September, the deputy director-general of the Ghana Atomic Energy Commission announced the International Atomic Energy Agency's agreement to assist Ghana in performing a training needs assessment for its nuclear capacity. On 7 October, Ghana signed a memorandum of understanding with Brazil to construct a 9,000 MW capacity hydroelectric dam on the River Oti, at Juallay near Pwalugu in the Upper East Region. On 20 November, the Volta River Authority (VRA) confirmed that the West African Gas Pipeline Company would deliver enough gas to power the VRA's 110 MW turbines and distribute *energy* supplies in Ghana. Furthermore, Ghana progressed with plans to supply its own natural gas, and announced on 4 October the selection of Nigeria-based Oando as a partner to the Ghana National Petroleum Corporation (GNPC), to develop the natural gas infrastructure from the offshore Jubilee Oilfields, a project worth $ 1 bn. The VRA also announced plans on 23 November to establish a wind farm in Ada that would add 50 MW–80 MW of electricity to the national grid.

Oil prospecting became the busiest hub of the energy sector and several institutions, both national and international, called for transparency and accountability. The new administration therefore took comprehensive steps to streamline the initiatives of the previous government. On 27 February, Mills announced the government's decision to review the previous government's draft oil law in order to ensure the better regulation and transparency of oil deals. Kosmos Energy's stake in the Jubilee Oilfields was alleged to have been negotiated under a deal too generous for the national interest, and became subject to investigation. On 9 March, the Revenue Watch Institute congratulated the Mills administration on its decision to publicly disclose all present and future contracts with oil companies and expressed the hope that Ghana would incorporate the oil sector into the Ghana Extractive Industries Transparency Initiative. On 29 September, Mills met with World Bank President Robert Zoellick in Washington DC and announced plans to set up a growth fund to manage oil revenues. On 12 October, the president announced that a petroleum revenue management bill was being drafted to ensure prudent use of the expected revenue from the oil and gas sectors. Finance Minister Kwabena Duffuor announced on 18 November that the government would establish an oil industrialisation plan to ensure judicious application of the expected revenues. International interest in Ghana's oil industry also arose. On 13 July, India's state-run

Oil and Natural Gas Corporation expressed interest in putting in a formal bid to buy a 30% stake in the Jubilee Oilfields. On 20 September, the GNPC announced plans to collaborate with the China National Oil Offshore Corporation to provide the GNPC with financial and technical support in exploration.

The Corporate Social Responsibility Movement organised a two-day meeting from 17 March for stakeholders in the oil and gas industries to discuss the ecological and economic impacts of oil production. The fishing industry was particularly concerned and the director of petroleum at the ministry of energy pledged to set up a team to examine the concerns of the fisheries sector. The universities have been no exception to the impact of the *oil boom*, and on 4 March, Brong Ahafo Regional Minister Kwadwo Nyamekye Marfo reaffirmed government commitment to upgrade the Faculty of Forest Resource Technology of the Kwame Nkrumah University of Science and Technology (KNUST) in Sunyani to a fully-fledged University of Energy and Natural Resources. On 27 August, the GNPC's communications manager announced that there had been a huge increase in the number of geology students graduating from KNUST, from 15 to 100 per year. On 9 November, the dean of the Engineering Faculty of the University of Ghana announced that the premier university was holding discussions with oil companies about training the requisite human resources.

The Tema Oil Refinery (TOR) suffered a string of shutdowns due to technical faults. The TOR refines about 45,000 barrels of oil, i.e. 75% of the daily consumption of 76,500 barrels. It was estimated that capacity should increase to about 145,000 barrels to meet national demand. Plans were therefore announced for the building of new refineries. The TOR's capacity problems became politically sensitive as they helped to push up *petrol prices* – a hot campaign issue for the new government. On 9 March, the government's National Petroleum Authority (NPA) made a political move and effected decreases in fuel prices at a total cost of almost $ 50 m in government subsidies. The government subsequently bowed to the global crude market and an IMF requirement to halt the subsidies. A series of petrol price hikes then occurred, culminating in a 5% price increase by the NPA in October.

As *job creation*, especially for young people, was a hot campaign issue, the 19 November budget statement announced that 14,700 jobs would be created for masons, carpenters and other skilled workers by the massive school building programme outlined above. On 25 November, it was announced that the National Youth Employment Programme (NYEP) was launching its recruitment drive for 2009/2010 to create productive employment opportunities in all sectors of the economy, and that it had plans to recruit 44,000 young people by December. The Youth in Agriculture module of the NYEP was also expected to recruit 50,000 young people by December. On 30 November, the deputy minister of lands and natural resources, Henry Kamel, announced in parliament that 30,000 jobs were to be created in 100 districts through the implementation of a National Forest Plantation Development Programme. Some 100 targeted districts were to benefit, with 300 jobs each. The government therefore still had some way to go in making an impact on the job creation front, particularly at the grass-roots level, where the pinch of the credit crunch was felt the most, and to which constituency the election promises had been directed.

There were *floods* during the year, which displaced a number of citizens of northern Ghana, damaging large areas of farmland and crops, and stretching national and UN relief services.

Ghana in 2010

Michael Amoah

The year saw Ghana achieve the status of oil drilling nation, alongside discussions on whether crude oil reserves could be used to secure loans. Cutting down on public debt became a headache as the state could not live within its means, but the GDP target was achieved. A series of disbursements from the IMF and World Bank contributed to budget support and development. It was a tough but productive year. The new administration was firmly in the saddle, but had to handle one domestic crisis after another. The president introduced the Better Ghana Agenda during his 25 January state of the nation address, and later organised a two-day retreat for the cabinet to strategise on delivering it. There was a constitutional review and a census. Developmental interest from the international community increased.

Domestic Politics

On 15 December, Ghana began oil production from the Golden Jubilee Fields. National concern about what to do with oil revenues generated acute attention to the *petroleum revenue management bill*. Clause 5, which was intended to prevent the use of the petroleum account and proven oil reserves as collateral security for loans, was removed by a parliamentary amendment.

On 11 January, President John Atta Mills inaugurated the Constitutional Review Committee, which conducted a constitutional survey in June. A variety of issues tested the *justice system* across the board, and challenged both Chief Justice Georgina

 | DOI 10.1163/9789004308183_008

Wood and Attorney General Betty Mould-Iddrisu personally. The failure of the latter's office to prosecute certain individuals from previous administrations in matters of wilfully causing financial loss to the state generated political talk. The end-of-year government reshuffle moved the attorney general to head the ministry for education. She was replaced by Martin Amidu, who was minister for the interior and, incidentally, a deputy attorney general during the presidency of Jerry Rawlings. Notable in the new-year reshuffle was the appointment of Professor Kwesi Botchwey to the Economic Advisory Council, and his subsequent appointment on 6 October to chair the newly formed National Gas Development Task Force.

Despite the firm allocation of funding within the budget to implement the single spine salary structure for public sector workers, this policy faltered as a result of red tape and the inability of the Fair Wages and Salaries Commission to migrate teachers onto the new payment scheme. However, the *wages* commission announced on 28 May a 10% pay rise for all public sector workers, with effect from July 2010, even though a lot of teachers did not receive the remuneration due to them for the reasons already mentioned.

An extensive national debate ensued over the award of a major *housing project* to the engineering and construction consortium STX of South Korea, to deliver up to 300,000 housing units. Issues included lack of clarity about procurement of the funding. Stakeholders, such as the Institute of Architects, Institute of Planners, Institution of Engineers, Institution of Surveyors and the Real Estate Developers Association, argued that the houses might not be affordable to ordinary Ghanaians; that the contract should not benefit a foreign company but a national one in order to stimulate the Ghanaian economy; and that the terms of the contract were not in the national interest, as debt could be claimed in the form of crude oil despatches to South Korea. A final agreement was cleared by the attorney general in October. The deal with STX was signed on 14 December, three days after parliament successfully voted for the removal of Clause 5 of the Petroleum Revenue Management Bill, leading the opposition to conclude that the STX deal would be financed from oil revenues.

It was reported in February that defaulting on payments by major electricity consumers, such as mining companies, industries and government departments, to the Volta River Authority (VRA), had resulted in under-recovery of the costs of electricity production, and financial distress to the VRA. A subsequent upward adjustment of *utility prices* by the Public Utility Regulatory Commission (PURC) became confused with the VRA's aim to recoup the losses. It generated uproar from consumers, and subsequently government intervention and funding to resolve the utility crisis. On 22 March, the VRA, the Electricity Company of Ghana (ECG) and the Ghana Grid Company (GRIDCo), announced a price increase from 12.77 Gp (Ghana pesewas) to 32.53 Gp per kw hour of electricity (100 Gp = GHS 1 [Ghana cedi]). The Ghana Water Company Limited also announced a price increase from 0.66 to 0.8 Gp per gallon of water. Huge concern already existed about illegal tapping of electricity, and the ECG initiated a drive in April to inspect up to 10,000 companies in Accra and Kumasi to expose this trend. Up to 13% of the ECG's power purchased from the VRA was lost through illegal connections, and amounted to an annual loss of GHS 78 m. On 27 May, parliament passed the PURC Amendment Bill to provide the relevant authorities with reliable funding and monitoring abilities.

However, simmering customer dissatisfaction with the utility price increase culminated in June and July with *protests* staged by consumer and trade organisations such as the Timber and Wood Workers Union, the Industrial and Commercial Workers Union, and eventually the overall Trades Union Congress (TUC), complemented by other actions by civil society organisations such as the Committee for Joint Action and the Alliance for Accountable Governance, all calling for a review of the utility tariffs. In response to these and many other petitions sent directly to the president, Vice President John Mahama was asked to chair a six-member committee that was formed on 29 July to review the tariffs. The committee, which comprised representatives of the Association of Ghana Industries, the TUC and PURC, revised the utility prices downwards. This was complemented by a government subsidy of GHS 185.8 m to absorb 10% of *electricity bills* across the board. The World Bank also provided $ 470 m as relief to the utility companies for several purposes, including the overhaul of utility sector infrastructure, water supplies and customer service. The government had earlier secured a loan facility totalling $ 520 m for the extension of electricity to 2,200 communities across the country: $ 350 m from the US Exim Bank and $ 170 m from the China Exim Bank. During the year, the VRA took measures to deal with the rising water levels at the Akosombo Dam and the Volta Lake Reservoir.

In July, the government refocused the National Development Planning Commission (NDPC) towards the Better Ghana Agenda, to formulate a development blueprint. A former presidential advisor to the caucus of the National Democratic Congress, Paul Victor Obeng, was appointed to chair the NDPC.

Incredibly, the well prepared and overdue national *census*, kicked off on 26 September, but somehow managed to experience a variety of hiccups in its implementation, including logistical and data challenges, despite the use of military personnel in its operations, and sufficient funding from the government and development partners to the tune of $ 50 m. The provisional census results put Ghana's population at 24,223,431.

Ethnic conflicts in northern Ghana continued with further incursions, arrests, recurrent curfews, peace negotiations and court dramas. The Bawku area experienced some more curfews, while the authorities sought ways of resolving the old conflict. In May, the National Disaster Management Organisation (NADMO) despatched relief items to people distressed and displaced by the renewed Bunkpurugu-Yunyoo conflict. The case of the existing Dagbon dispute between the rival Andani and Abudu factions went through the courts but was not concluded by year's end.

On 22 July, parliament ratified the African Charter on Democracy, Election and Governance.

Foreign Affairs

Ghana's foreign policy was tested for its loyalty to regional and sub-regional politics in connection with the post-electoral political impasse in *Côte d'Ivoire* and the onus on ECOWAS to intervene militarily. Ghana's cautious view that military intervention was not the solution in the heat of the moment initially seemed traitorous, but then prevailed as both ECOWAS and the AU went on to adopt the same position. It appeared that the sub-regional politics was more complex than generally understood. Ghana was already in talks with Côte d'Ivoire about oil and sea boundaries, and wished to avoid any escalation of tensions with neighbours. President Mills had already visited Côte d'Ivoire in October, as a follow-up to an earlier meeting in April between officials from both countries on the subject of boundaries. By sheer coincidence, Victor Gbeho, who was foreign policy advisor to the Ghanaian president, was in post as president of the ECOWAS Commission, having been elected in February. In the wake of the 28 November presidential elections, the main contention of Côte d'Ivoire's incumbent president, Laurent Gbagbo, was that the ambassadors of France and the US had met with the electoral commissioner, Youssouf

Bakayoko, immediately prior to his announcement of the electoral result that gave the victory to opposition leader Alassane Ouattara, giving rise to Gbagbo's contention that he was hoodwinked by international agents, who widely acclaimed Ouattara as the winner.

As crude oil supplies from Nigeria could not be guaranteed, President Mills visited *Equatorial Guinea* on 5 May to negotiate supplies, and mutual areas of cooperation in the fields of hydrocarbons, maritime transport, education, culture, fishing and the environment. President Mbasongo of Equatorial Guinea reciprocated with a four-day visit to Accra on 7–10 September.

The dispute over the attempted sale of oil stakes owned by US firm *Kosmos Energy*, which had been blocked by the Ghana National Petroleum Corporation and generated diplomatic tensions between the Ghanaian and US administrations, eventually reached a dignified conclusion after Kosmos appreciated that the host government was adamant about not acquiescing in dealings injurious to the national interest. The disputing parties reached a settlement just before Christmas. The US-Ghana Trade and Investment Framework Agreement Council had met in Accra on 2 July to discuss primary impediments and strategies to remove barriers and expand bilateral trade between the two countries. The 17-member US team was led by Florie Liser, assistant US trade representative. Trade between the US and Ghana increased by 48% to $ 1.3 bn.

In August, the fourth edition of the international military communication exercise 'African Endeavour 2010', which was initiated by the US Africa Command (*AFRICOM*) to build a strong and sustainable communication capability for African militaries in joint operations, took place in Accra, with 36 countries, two sub-regional organisations and three international bodies participating. Earlier, on 13 March, the US had presented four

speed patrol boats to the Ghana Navy, as part of the US Africa Partnership Station programme, which is a naval component of AFRICOM.

On 18 August, the energy commission announced China's grant of $ 300 m to extend electricity to rural communities in the Upper West, Upper East and Northern Regions. On 3 September, Vice President Mahama, attended UNCTAD's 2nd World Investment Forum held in Xiamen, China; the first forum was hosted by Ghana in April 2008. Mahama's visit was followed a couple of weeks later with a six-day official visit to *China* by President Mills, which led to deals worth up to $ 16 bn: (a) a $ 10.4 bn concessionary loan from the China Exim Bank to develop transport networks, including a railway system from Kumasi to Paga, and other sectors of the economy; (b) a $ 3 bn loan from the China Development Bank for Ghana's oil-and-gas sector, and a $ 400 m guarantee for water and e-governance projects; (c) a $ 1.2 bn deal with Bosai Minerals Group to build a bauxite and aluminium refinery in Ghana over four years (Bosai had already purchased from RIO Tinto Alcan an 80% share in the Ghana Bauxite Company); (d) an agreement with Shangai Construction Company to build two regional hospitals in Wa and Kumasi. However, on 16 December, Ghana's Food and Drugs Board revoked the registration licences of two Chinese companies for engaging in activities that were in contravention of Ghana's Food and Drugs Law.

The relationship between Ghana and *Brazil* was mutually strengthened on a number of fronts. On 31 March, both countries signed an agreement on laboratory procedures in biotechnology and genetic resource management, which enables research by Ghana's Council for Scientific and Industrial Research to reduce diseases that affect cassava and to introduce new varieties. Mahama's visit to Brazil in April led to a deal for the Dias Branco Group of Companies to set up a $ 300 m biscuit and pasta factory in Ghana. Brazil also agreed credit to acquire a 90-seater

ERJ190 jet for the Ghana air force, manufactured by the Brazilian Aeronautics Company Embraer. On 3 September, Ghana's PBC Shea Limited announced a $ 10 m investment to process sheanuts into butter for export to Brazil. Ghana obtained a $ 500 m Brazilian facility to construct a dam in Pwalugu in the Upper East Region to accommodate the excess water spillage from the Bagre Dam in neighbouring Burkina Faso, and to cater for another flood-related dam in the Western Region. In November, Brazil granted $ 13.7 m to Ghana's Sickle Cell Foundation for the construction of a Blood and Sickle Cell Centre in Kumasi, in response to a Brazil-Ghana Technical Cooperation Agreement in Sickle Cell Disease signed at the fifth Brazilian International Symposium on Sickle Cell Disease in Belo Horizonte.

On 9 July, the EU disbursed € 41.8 m through the Multi-Donor Budget Support (MDBS) Framework, under the MDGs Contract and Food Facility instrument. On 28 September, Ghana's ministry of finance, the German Technical Cooperation (GTZ) and the Swiss Secretariat of Economic Affairs together signed a Memorandum of Understanding in which *Germany* and *Switzerland* jointly committed a € 2.1 m grant facility to support Ghana's reforms in tax policy and administration. On 28 October, the German ambassador to Ghana, Eberhard Schanze, handed over completed building projects and educational equipment worth € 0.5 m to the Electrical and Mechanical Engineering Technical Training School of the Ghana Armed Forces. On 5 November, Ghana and Germany signed a financial cooperation agreement worth € 107.5 m (approximately GHS 196 m) covering the period 2010–2012, in the following priority areas of cooperation: agriculture; sustainable economic development; decentralization; and MDBS contribution. On 10 December, Germany donated 182 computers and accessories worth € 0.15 m to the ministry of food and agriculture to help in the retrieval of data and statistical information on agriculture.

In late February, Russian oil firm LukOil announced a significant oil find off the shores of Ghana. On 2 July, the Russian trade and economic attaché in Accra, Evgeny Tereshenchenko, announced over 30 scholarships for Ghanaian students to study in *Russia*. In A[illegible] joint trade delegation from Russia and *Belarus* including five ministers of State, came to meet President Mills to discuss trilateral investment cooperation. They were led by Anatoly Tkachuk, vice president of the Russian Union of Industrialists and Entrepreneurs, and Viktor Sheiman, special affairs assistant to the president of the Belarus Republic.

On 15 March, the Ghana Stock Exchange, the Nigerian Stock Exchange, and the 'Bourse Régionale des Valeurs Mobilières' of Côte d'Ivoire agreed to integrate their capital markets into the *West African Securities Markets*; four organisations were granted observer status: ECOWAS, the West African Monetary Institute, the UEMOA, and the Sierra Leone Stock Exchange. On 30 November, parliament gave its approval for Ghana to join the African Finance Corporation, a public-private partnership investment bank established by Nigeria, Ghana, Gambia and Guinea Bissau. Ghana joined with $ 50 m, which secures a seat on the board.

A second batch of 50 immigration officers from the Liberian Bureau of Immigration and Naturalization (BIN), comprising 40 men and ten women, arrived in Ghana on 14 May to begin a three-month training course, as part of a tripartite project agreement between Ghana, *Liberia* and The Netherlands that would facilitate the enlistment of the participants into Liberia's BIN.

On 23 July, GRIDCo announced a Ghana-Burkina Faso project to construct a 225 kW transmission line from a Bolgatanga substation to Zagtouli in Burkina Faso, as part of the West Africa Power Pool Project. The cost of this power transmission project is estimated at $ 75 m, and transmission capacity is expected to be raised to 100 MW by 2015. The ECOWAS Regional Electricity

Regulatory Authority (ERERA) was launched in Accra on 9 November as an independent entity to regulate *cross-border trade in electricity* and provide support to national regulators of the electricity sector in West Africa. ERERA oversees the development and monitoring of uniform technical rules for managing exchanges between interconnected systems to maximize their technical efficiency; the countries involved are Burkina Faso, Côte d'Ivoire, Ghana, Togo, Benin, Nigeria, Niger, Mali, Guinea, Senegal, and Mauritania, which ceased to be part of ECOWAS in 2000.

Ghana welcomed Crown Prince Naruhito of *Japan* for a three-day official visit from 7 March, which was reciprocated with a four-day official visit by President Mills to Japan at the end of September. On 21 June, *Angola*'s President Jose Eduardo dos Santos, and the first lady of Angola, paid a two-day visit to Ghana, to enhance bilateral ties.

Ghana also played host to a number of *international events*, including: the first international women's fair, which was held in Accra on 28–30 May; the 8th West African Mining and Power Conference, which began in Accra on 26 May; the World Glaucoma Summit in Accra on 6 August; the 10th African Tax Administration Forum hosted by the Ghana Revenue Authority (GRA) on 4–8 October; the four nations (Ghana Nigeria, Benin and Togo) Co-Prosperity Alliance Zone seminar, hosted in Accra on 28 October; and the launching of ERERA in Accra on 9 November.

Socioeconomic Developments

The 6.5% GDP *growth* target was nearly achieved at 6%. Inflation, which stood at 14.8% in January fell remarkably to 8.58% in December. On 19 February, the Bank of Ghana's monetary policy committee cut the interest rate to 16%, and reduced it further to

13.5% on 16 July. However, the government struggled to keep to the budget deficit reduction target of 7.5%. In June, the fiscal deficit for the first half of the year stood at 5.3% of GDP, and the IMF warned that expenditure commitments and debts were unsustainable, particularly in view of the size of the wage bill. The deficit rose to 9.7% by July, and public debt was forecast or expected to rise to 62%. The Centre for Policy Analysis revealed in October that the $ 10.3 bn public debt stock for June was more than the $ 9.3 bn for the same period the previous year. The total public debt at the end of the year was $ 11.8 bn or 38.6% of GDP. However, remittances to Ghana between January and May amounted to $ 4.2 bn, and represented a 22% increase on the same period the previous year. Furthermore, reforms in *revenue collection* resulted in GHS 5.9 bn being collected by the GRA, and a target of GHS 7.5 bn was set for 2011. On 14 May, the GHS 2 bank note was issued.

On 10 June, the *IMF* approved a $ 119 m loan, which increased Ghana's total disbursements under the ECF to $ 218 m. The IMF warned that reducing the deficit involved tighter spending controls and more revenue mobilization. On 28 June, the World Bank approved $ 44.7 m from the IDA as additional funding for the ongoing eGhana Project. This was followed in July by another World Bank approval, which released the second and last tranche of $ 143 m of the Economic Governance and Poverty Reduction Credit. The World Bank waived the benchmark of cabinet approval for the Ghana Petroleum Regulatory Authority, and oil and gas fiscal regime legislations, because on-going debates on these matters had shown significantly divergent views, which needed to be reconciled to establish a nationally owned legal framework to govern the oil and gas industry in future. The drive to amend the petroleum revenue management bill in order to collaterise crude oil may have arisen from the waiving of this benchmark. The government, however, progressed with the Freedom of Information

Bill as part of extending legislation on the Extractive Industry Transparency Initiative (EITI) to Ghana's *oil and gas sector,* and achieved EITI compliance status.

Other funding approved by the *World Bank* included: $ 70 m additional financing for the Ghana Energy and Access Project; $ 88.6 m for the Social Opportunities Project; $ 25 m for the Second Agriculture Development Policy Operation; $ 10 m for the Third Natural Resources and Environmental Governance; $ 75 m for the Sustainable Rural Water and Sanitation Project; and $ 257.5 m for the Abidjan-Lagos Trade and Transport Facilitation Project. Finally, in December, the World Bank Board approved a credit line of $ 38 m for the implementation of the Oil and Gas Capacity Building Project (OGCBP). This concessional loan had a repayment period of 35 years and a ten-year grace period, and constituted two-thirds of the total cost of the project. Ghana and Norway are the other co-financiers. The OGCBP was planned to take off in 2011 and end in 2015.

The Ghana Investment Promotion Centre announced that *foreign direct investment* (FDI) had doubled to $ 1.11 bn. The year ended with 385 projects at a total estimated value of $ 1.3 bn. The FDI component of this figure was $ 1.1 bn, a significant increase in comparison with $ 551.3 m recorded in 2009. With regard to the number of projects, China came top with 67 registered projects, but with respect to estimated project costs, China came fourth, behind Bermuda, Nigeria and Trinidad.

Ghana Chamber of Mines data showed that revenues from *gold* exports for the first half of the year rose by 31% from $ 1,288 m in 2009 to $ 1,683 m. Diamond production also climbed 14%, while revenues more than doubled, from $ 2.8 m in 2009 to $ 6.9 m. Bauxite output rose, and earnings jumped 41% from $ 6.3 m in 2009 to $ 8.8 m. Manganese output rose, and revenues increased from $ 28.1 m in 2009 to $ 37.2 m. Bank of Ghana data show that exports of *cocoa* and related products for the first part of the year amounted to $ 1,300 m, a 22.6% increase compared with $ 1,060 m in 2009. The cocoa harvest for the full season of 2009/10 was 944,000 tonnes, up by 34% from the previous year's figure of 703,000 tonnes. The national producer price of cocoa rose by 33% from GHS 2,400 to GHS 3,200 per tonne, with effect from 1 October. The price of a 64-kilo bag of cocoa was also fixed at GHS 200 to discourage smuggling. Up to 60,000 tonnes of cocoa were reportedly lost through smuggling to neighbouring Côte d'Ivoire and Togo during the season. During the 82nd regular session of the International Cocoa Organisation held in London on 13–17 September, the chief executive of the Ghana Cocoa Board, Anthony Fofie, was elected to chair the governing council of the world body for the 2010/11 cocoa year.

To ensure *food security*, the ministry of finance released GHS 27.2 m in April to accumulate a buffer stock of food supplies: GHS 15.2 m to refurbish food storage facilities and warehouses; GHS 10 m to provide a fertiliser subsidy for farmers; and GHS 2.1 m to upgrade dams for irrigation. At the end of the first quarter, some storage facilities of the Ghana Food Distribution Corporation at Wenchi had been completed, and there were similar silos in Nkoranza and Sekye-Dumasi. On 28 September, the food and agriculture minister announced a 5% increase in food supply, and launched the Medium-Plan Agriculture Sector Investment Plan. On 31 August, the country representative of the International Centre for Soil Fertility and Agricultural Development announced a three-year project financed by the Alliance for Green Revolution in Africa to cover about 50,000 smallholders cultivating maize, rice, sorghum and soybeans in the Northern, Upper East and West Regions. The project would address marketing and post-harvest problems affecting farmers, and develop commercial relationships with industrial processors, the Ghana School Feeding

Programme, WFP, local entrepreneurs, and urban consumers in southern Ghana. On 3 September, former UN Secretary-General Kofi Annan opened the African Green Revolution Forum in Accra. A Friends of the Earth report was issued, which published a list of foreign companies that had obtained significant portions of land for the cultivation of biofuels, chiefly jatropha.

On 13 March, Vice President Mahama led a Ghanaian delegation to participate in the 6th Annual Confederation of Indian Industries Conclave. Deals struck included: (a) an agreement signed with Mihindra Company Limited to supply 1,000 *tractors* to Ghanaian farmers and set up a servicing and training plant to complement the existing one in Kumasi; (b) an agreement signed with Kirloskar Brothers Limited, a multi-Purpose Engineering Company, to upgrade all existing irrigation facilities and consider building new ones; and (c) an expression of interest by Gas Authority India Limited in establishing a *fertilizer* factory in Ghana, to be sited at Shama in the Western Region. A Memorandum of Understanding was later signed on 6 July to form a partnership to tap into Ghana's commercial gas exploration to feed the fertilizer venture.

The President's *Malaria* Initiative (PMI) collaborated with the US embassy to expand indoor residual spraying from five to eight districts in the Northern Region, covering 141,621 households with over 708,000 people. Under this initiative, USAID provided 955,000 insecticide-treated nets for distribution in the Northern and Eastern Regions, and donated items valued at $ 5.7 m to the Ghana Health Service on 4 May. On 8 November, the Food and Drugs Board directed the recall of sub-standard anti-malarial medicines from circulation by their manufacturers and importers, and required them to submit a recall report within ten days.

On 27 March, the government initiated the roll-out of a GHS 45 m programme to construct six-unit classroom blocks and dormitories for each of 495 *senior high schools*, to guarantee accommodation for students due for admission in the 2010–11 academic year. In April, the government suspended payment of the salaries of 2,383 'ghost' teachers on the payroll. Both the director-general of the education service and the national coordinator of the school feeding programme were sacked in the same month. In October, the Dutch government committed to a GHS 2.8 m grant to sponsor a Social Accountability Project aimed at addressing some of the challenges facing the Ghana School Feeding Programme. On 27 May, the Ghana Education Trust Fund released GHS 3 m to the Council for Technical and Vocational Education to support apprenticeship training in the informal sector. On the same day, the Commission on Human Rights and Administrative Justice embarked on human rights *education* for basic schools in the Ga South area of the Greater Accra Region as part of its public education mandate.

On 13 June, 22 professionals and students from the University of Ghana (UG), working on environmental and related issues, participated in an exchange programme with the University of Duquesne in Pittsburgh, Pennsylvania, on how to manage complex environmental and social challenges arising from the extraction of natural resources such as oil and minerals. The programme was coordinated by Dr George Wiafe, a lecturer at UG's oceanography department. On 17 August, a two-day international conference on educational access, quality and outcomes in Africa, opened at the University of Cape Coast (UCC). In September, the construction of facilities to upgrade the Cape Coast regional hospital began in order to enable UCC's *medical school* to undertake clinical work at a local hospital. Also, Takoradi Polytechnic collaborated with the Aircraft Maintenance Training Institute and the Cincinnati-based Afrimeric Engineering International to introduce aircraft technician courses.

In addition to responding to the now familiar *flooding* in northern Ghana caused by spillages from the Bagre Dam in Burkina Faso, NADMO handled several instances of flood that caused havoc in southern Ghana across the year. A Presidential Task Force Committee on Floods now exists to handle disaster relief and resettlements.

The Ghana Tourist Board organised a paragliding festival at Kwahu Atibie on 2–5 April.

Ghana in 2011

Michael Amoah

Flourishing oil sales in the first year of commercial drilling propelled GDP into double figures, even though the national debt also increased. There was single-figure end-of-year inflation for the second time in two years. Two petroleum related acts of parliament were passed, and a national gas company was formed. Petrol price increases were very well managed. Citizens were also rewarded with other real benefits of cocoa, apart from foreign exchange. Ghana continued to negotiate sensitive foreign policy curves with neighbours and others abroad. Sufficient funds were committed for the prosecution of a competent election in 2012, and the nation progressed with the agenda of bridging the gap in development between the north and the south.

Domestic Politics

On 1 January, President John Atta Mills declared a "year of action". Despite the previous intensive debate on the *Petroleum Revenue Management Act* and crude oil as collateral for loans, the government expedited action for a $ 3 bn loan from the China Development Bank but on terms of doubtful benefit to the national interest, according to the opposition, citing the potential granting of the right to 90 crude oil liftings of 950,000 barrels per lifting at $ 85 a barrel over 20 years. The Revenue Management Act was passed on 2 March, and the Petroleum Commission Bill also passed into law on 1 June. Subsequently, the government presented arguments against IMF and World Bank reservations

 | DOI 10.1163/9789004308183_009

regarding the Chinese loan, such as the unwillingness of the West to fund the infrastructure Ghana needed.

A *Petroleum Security Co-ordinating Committee* was set up in January and four new armoured speed boats were subsequently added to the Western Naval Command closest to the oil waters. Two Airbus Military C295 transports, an Embraer 190 and two Diamond DA 42 surveillance aircraft were also ordered. A CASA C-295-M twin-turboprop transport aircraft was commissioned to replace the Fokker 27 that had been in use for 37 years. The ministry of food and agriculture (MOFA) funded two 46 m. patrol vessels for fisheries surveillance and combating piracy and towards the general drive to modernise the navy and beef up maritime security against external threats.

Following the July report of the National Task Force on Gas chaired by Dr Kwesi Botchway, the president authorised the formation of the National Gas Company. The *Tema Oil Refinery* faced financial challenges, and the price of petrol went up in December. However, all actors including government, the banking sector, road transport operators, legal institutions and the refinery itself acted amicably to avoid chaos. A Petroleum Commission Board was set up in November by the minister of energy to execute cost efficiency and sustainability measures. The New Alpha Refinery-Ghana, the Ghanaian subsidiary of the South African company, undertook feasibility studies for establishing a tank farm, an oil refinery and a gas turbine power-generation plant, which would have the capacity to process 200,000 b/d of crude *oil*, well over the 45,000 b/d currently produced by the existing refinery.

The National Tripartite Committee increased the minimum wage from GHS 3.11 to GHS 3.73 from 15 February. There were frequent demonstrations by civil service labour unions about distortions in the migration of salary structures onto the single spine salary scheme being administered by the Fair Wages and

Salaries Commission. On 8 October, public health doctors of the Ghana Medical Association (GMA) embarked on *strike action* for over two weeks, causing the president to abort his October trip to the Commonwealth Heads of Government Meeting in Australia. There were reports that some middle-level government officials earned more than doctors, who worked sacrificial hours to save lives, but the ruling of a compulsory arbitration panel to which the case was referred did not address all the concerns of the GMA.

Laureta Vivian Lamptey was sworn in on 1 August as head of the Commission for Human Rights and Administrative Justice, replacing Anna Bossman, who resigned to take on an international assignment. While the television industry progressed with the digital switchover project, some key sackings rocked the *media*. On 15 April, the general manager of the Ghana News Agency (GNA) was sacked by the National Media Commission (NMC). William Ampem Darko, the director-general of the Ghana Broadcasting Corporation, who had also been sacked by the NMC, was effectively replaced in mid-October by Berifi Appenteng. The existing board of the Electricity Company of Ghana (ECG) was dissolved on 1 December, and another reconstituted later.

Strong demands from the opposition parties for the verification of voters on election day to complement the biometric registration of voters generated intense debate between the Electoral Commission and its Inter Party Advisory Committee. The crucial nature of the *2012 elections* required that the electoral process be satisfactory to all parties, so the finance minister committed sufficient funds to cover such verification.

The government did not bow to pressure from the US and UK governments over *gay rights issues*, regardless of whether this might be tied to aid. Parliament rejected the legalisation of homosexuality and resolved to maintain the country's criminal code in line with the constitution.

On 23 December, Ghana announced that it would review the ECOWAS protocol on *Fulanis*. The herdsmen had encroached on areas of land in Agogo to graze their cattle, assuming the territory to be available so that they could pursue their nomadic life-style. It was alleged that the herdsmen also struck up relationships with the wives of some Agogo townsfolk. The consequent unrest led to the intervention of a combined military and police force, which escorted the nomads to a new area allocated to them.

Foreign Affairs

A great deal occurred on the *ECOWAS* front. Minister of Environment, Science and Technology Sherry Ayittey was appointed on 17 May to the board of the ECOWAS Regional Centre for Renewable Energy and Energy Efficiency. On 30 August, the ECG led on the West African Power Pool (WAPP) project, and signed a GHS 3.6 m deal with its Togolese counterpart 'Communauté Electrique du Benin', to supply power to communities in neighbouring Togo. Under WAPP, the Volta River Authority (VRA) is also expected to supply to Burkina Faso and Côte d'Ivoire with a minimum 2 MW of electricity each.

A mutiny and military clashes in *Burkina Faso* during April caused the closure of both sides of the Burkinabè/Ghanaian border. Ghana's ambassador to Burkina Faso was also attacked. At the beginning of July, after a three-day conference to strengthen trans-border cooperation and peaceful coexistence, the governor of Central East Burkina Faso, the district chief executive of Savannah Region of Togo, and Ghana's Upper East regional minister signed a joint communiqué. On 14 August, the Ghanaian Police and Togolese Gendarmerie conducted a joint operation against suspected criminal hideouts along the Ghana-Togo frontier at Aflao, which led to the arrest of 33 suspects. It was reported on 26 September that Ghana and *Togo* had agreed to settle outstanding claims of CFAfr 36 m incurred between the two countries under the ECOWAS Brown Card Insurance scheme. On 3 October, a six-member delegation on a three-day working visit from Togo's constitutional court called on Ghana's Chief Justice Georgina Wood in Accra, and discussed mutual court structures and jurisdictional roles with Ghanaian colleagues.

On 21 June, a four-man transport delegation from *Liberia*, led by their deputy minister of transport, Ebenezer Kolliegbo, visited Accra to make strategic decisions. In September, 40 Liberian immigration officers graduated from the Ghana Immigration Academy and Training School in Assin Fosu. It was noted in mid-December that over 11,000 Liberian refugees were due to return to a now stable Liberia in 2012.

On 18 July, the West Africa Network for Peace Building revealed that weapons from the *Côte d'Ivoire* crisis had appeared in Ghana. On 10 September in Abuja, Nigeria, a mini summit of ECOWAS heads of state from Senegal, Nigeria, Ghana, Côte d'Ivoire and Liberia discussed arms proliferation. On 6 October, Ivorian President Alassane Ouattarra held closed-door talks with President Mills in Accra, and on 7 October, the Ghanaian president held another closed-door session with the ECOWAS chair, Nigerian President Goodluck Jonathan, in Accra. Consequently, Ghana, Côte d'Ivoire and UNHCR signed a tripartite agreement on 7 October on the voluntary repatriation of 18,000 Ivorian refugees. The two countries agreed to engage UNHCR to repatriate refugees identified as ex-combatants to a third country that did not border on Côte d'Ivoire. Relations between Côte d'Ivoire and Liberia, which share a common border, became strained because of Ivorian (or former president Gbagbo's) support for the Movement for Democracy in Liberia during the second Liberian civil war of 1999–2003. An attempt was made in 2010 by Liberian President

Ellen Johnson-Sirleaf to repair the relationship, but sensitivities remained in certain Ivorian quarters. On 7 December, the new Ivorian government sent warrants to Ghana for the extradition of alleged Ivorian ex-combatants, coinciding with the Ivorian government's 29 November unveiling of a new and controversial *maritime border* with Ghana, which sought to incorporate a substantial area of Ghana's Jubilee Oilfields. Taking into account the indisputable accuracy of modern GPS technology, and the ongoing discussions between the two countries in accordance with the UN Convention on the Law of the Sea (which followed the ECOWAS agreement that had resulted from a ministerial meeting on 13–14 February 2009), this new development on oil boundaries seemed politically motivated.

On 7 February, the Australian High Commissioner announced scholarship awards to 26 Ghanaian students, to pursue Masters degrees in *Australia*. On 9 April, an 11-member delegation from private sector organisations of the Energy Chamber of *Trinidad and Tobago* arrived in Accra on a week-long visit to explore opportunities in the energy sector, and seek joint venture partners. On 25–27 April, Trinidad and Tobago's Minister of Energy Affairs Carolyn Seepersad-Bachan discussed Ghana's Gas Infrastructure Development Project with Energy Minister Joe Oteng-Adjei and government officials. The National Gas Company of Trinidad and Tobago was then invited to conclude joint venture negotiations with the Ghana National Petroleum Corporation.

In May, the *US* Embassy handed over the American Corner Research Library to the Legon Centre for International Affairs and Diplomacy (LECIAD), to serve as a nerve centre for studying US foreign policy, educational system, culture and history. The director of LECIAD, Professor Kwame Boafo-Arthur, reiterated that the library provided opportunities for researchers. At the beginning of June, US Senators Johnny Isakson of Georgia and Chris Coons of

Delaware visited Ghana to assess the state of projects under phase one of the Millennium Challenge Account.

On 2 June, Ghana's Vice President John Mahama and cabinet colleagues, and the EU Ambassador to Ghana Claude Maerten and eight EU ambassadors based in Accra, met in Accra under the framework of political dialogue defined in the *Cotonou Agreement*, to take stock of issues of mutual interest in both Europe and Ghana.

On 8 September, Sharon Bar-Li presented her Letters of Credence to the president of Ghana in Accra, to mark the first posting of an *Israeli* ambassador to Ghana for three decades.

Accra saw a variety of other *international events* and visits. On 15 March, a delegation from the UN Industrial Development Organization came for a two-day conference on diversifying African economies. On 30 March, *Spain*'s Secretary of State for Foreign and Iberoamerican Affairs Juan Antonio Yya Fez-Barnuevo commenced an official visit to Ghana and, in April, the third symposium of the African Forum for Agricultural Advisory Services was held. On 16 August, President Ian Khama of *Botswana* held bilateral talks with President Mills and, on 27 October, the UN Fund for Population Activities launched the 2011 edition of the World Population Report. In addition, Minister for Tourism the Honourable Akua Dansua was appointed to the advisory board of the Institute for Cultural Diplomacy in Berlin on 1 April, and President Mills visited *Canada* in November, and held closed-door discussions in Ottawa with Canadian Prime Minister Stephen Harper.

Socioeconomic Developments

According to the Ghana Statistical Service, Ghana earned $ 444,124,724 from 3,930,189 barrels of crude oil, propelling *GDP* to

14.4%, far above the 5.1% target. A non-oil GDP target of 7.6% was set for 2012. The economy also experienced single digit *inflation*, ending at 8.6% (the same as in 2010). An 8.5% target was set for 2012. Total public debt at the end of the year stood at $ 14 bn or 44.2% of GDP (a rise of 34.1% compared with the previous year). Overall fiscal operations saw revenue and grants amounting to GHS 10.7 bn, compared with GHS 7.5 bn in 2010, but total expenditure was GHS 12.7 bn, compared with GHS 9.2 bn in 2010. Public service wage and salary increases shot up from just over GHS 2 bn to GHS 5.2 bn. The Bank of Ghana announced that the "narrow" budget deficit arising from wage increases was financed by issuing domestic bonds. A sum of GHS 30 m was allocated from the Oil Fund to support the Forestry Commission for plantation development and afforestation. On 24 January, the British High Commission announced a £ 36 m DFID grant for Multi-Donor Budget Support (MDBS). Also under MDBS, the EU disbursed € 26.4 m on 14 August, in the context of the MDG contract. On 2 March, Ghana and Japan signed two budget support agreements: $ 2.4 m for Ghana's health sector, and $ 12 m for food aid for victims of the 2010 flood.

On 22 January, the *World Bank* approved a $ 215 m Poverty Reduction Support Credit, to help consolidate fiscal stabilisation and promote development objectives of the Ghana Shared Growth and Development Agenda, which is the medium-term development policy framework for 2010–2013. On 16 March, the World Bank, in partnership with DFID, the European Commission and the Danish International Development Agency (DANIDA), signed a memorandum of understanding to pool a $ 60 m grant over four years for the implementation of the Ghana Integrated Financial Management Information System. In June, the World Bank and the Canadian International Development Agency voted $ 17 m to assist combating desertification and drought. In July, the World Bank announced an offer of $ 3.86 m to the Accra

Metropolitan Assembly in support of its Millennium City Project. In August, the government acquired $ 40 m from the World Bank to provide technical and financial support for the Ghana Statistics Development Plan: $ 30 m came from IDA Credit and $ 10 m from the Statistics for Results Facility Catalytic Fund. In October, an *IMF* team led by Christina Daseking conducted the fifth economic review under the ECF arrangement since June. It was reported that this review had implications for Ghana's authority to proceed with a $ 3 bn loan application with China. In December, the World Bank announced that it was committing $ 50 m to the second phase of Ghana's Land Administration Project.

The Ghana Investment Promotion Centre announced *FDI* worth $ 7.68 bn, of which $ 2.5 bn attributed to the beleaguered STX project and $ 3 bn from the Asanteman Home Group Ltd were yet to be realised. The $ 2.18 bn already in the bag, was well over the set target of $ 1.5 bn, which had been exceeded by the third quarter of the year. Altogether, 514 new projects were registered, of which China continued to dominate with 79, followed by India with 77, Nigeria 39 and Lebanon 36. With regard to amounts invested, the high value of STX meant that South Korea topped the list with $ 4.77 bn, followed by Bermuda, the value of whose investments was recorded as $ 300 m. Following the official listing of Tullow Oil Plc in July, the Ghana Stock Exchange became the third largest capital market in sub-Saharan Africa, after South Africa and Nigeria.

The Chamber of Mines reported a 3% rise in *gold* production in the first half of the year from 1,455,234 ounces in the previous year to 1,497,023 ounces. Gold revenues in the same period increased by 31% from $ 1,683 m to $ 2,205 m. Ghana sold a 1.3% stake in AngloGold Ashanti for $ 43.97 a share, which generated $ 215 m in government revenue. *Diamond* revenues in the first half of the year also increased by 42%, from $ 6.9 m in 2010 to $ 9.7 m, despite an 8% decline in production. A divestiture of the former Ghana Diamond Company resulted in a Ghanaian owned company now known as the Great Consolidated Diamond Ghana Limited.

The *cocoa* harvest for the full 2010/2011 season increased from 944,000 tonnes in 2010 to 1,024,000 tonnes. The Bank of Ghana reported that cocoa had already earned $ 1,900 m by the end of November. In response, the government announced an increase in the producer price of cocoa in October, from GHS 3,200 per tonne to GHS 3,280 for the 2011/2012 season. Cocoa farmers would then earn GHS 205 per bag of 64 kg, up from GHS 200. A series of other benefits arose from cocoa. On 25 July, the Cadbury Cocoa Partnership presented 10,000 household solar lanterns valued at GHS 600,000 for distribution to cocoa farmers in 160 communities. On 8 September, COCOBOD inaugurated a 64-Slice CT Scanner for the Cocoa Clinic in Accra. On 8 October, Clement Bugase, the chief executive officer (CEO) of the Community Water and Sanitation Agency, announced that all residents of cocoa growing areas in the country would receive drinking water from solar water machines by the end of 2013. The GNA also announced on 22 December a COCOBOD release of $ 200 m to the ministry of roads and highways, under the Cocoa Roads Improvement Project (Tranche II), to carry out maintenance on 4,000 km of road and spot improvements on 2,000 km, and to surface 750 km of feeder roads with bitumen.

On 27 April, the VRA revealed that plans were in place to increase access to *electricity* from 60% to 90% of the population. On 29 August, the Public Utilities Regulatory Commission announced a 7% increase in electricity tariffs and a 6.7% increase in water tariffs from 1 September to 30 November. A subsequent 3% increase in the electricity tariff, and a 1.1% increase in the water tariff were introduced on 1 December. The Sunon Asogli power plant produced 15% of total electricity generated.

On 20 March, the government announced it had secured $ 80 m to undertake infrastructural development in polytechnics, with the aim of generating skills to sustain Ghana's middle-income economy status. On 17 June, the government announced the release of GHS 2 m for bursaries and scholarships for over 5,000 qualified applicants to second-cycle vocational, technical and tertiary institutions under the Mathematics, Science and Technology Scholarships Scheme for the 2011/12 academic year. On 22 July, the minister of education announced the introduction of an annual free apprenticeship programme for junior high school graduates unable to continue their *education* to enable them to acquire employable skills. The pilot scheme would sponsor 5,000 beneficiaries through informal apprenticeships. The temporarily suspended school feeding programme resumed on 19 September. A total of 791 students from less affluent schools were admitted to the University of Cape Coast for the 2011/2012 academic year, representing 18% of total admissions to the university. On 13 July, The Netherlands provided € 2 m for the implementation of the 'Girl Child Project', to be carried out by four civil society organisations, the Sissala Literacy and Development Programme, the Centre for the Alleviation of Poverty and Child Support, the Ark Foundation, and the CRESCENT organisation. They signed a memorandum of understanding to implement the project over five years and announced that it sought to empower young schoolgirls aged ten to 17 and young women aged 18 to 24 who did not attend school.

On 18 January, Ghana signed an agreement with OPUS 7 SRO Satov of Austria for the construction of 12 district hospitals and technical training institutions, and the supply of two air ambulances, 200 ambulance cars, 50 mobile clinics and ten educative mobile units. In March, an Oxfam report that criticised the operations of the National *Health* Insurance Authority was described by the authority's CEO as unsubstantiated and inaccurate. Also in March, President Mills ordered the release of GHS 5 m to fight a cholera outbreak. In July, the World Bank commended the Northern Regional office of the Ghana AIDS Commission and its social partners for successfully implementing the Multi-Sectoral HIV/AIDS Programme, funded by the World Bank over five years and aimed at building collaboration between social partners in the fight against HIV/AIDS through capacity building and other interventions. Through measures adopted by the Regional AIDS Commission, civil society organisations and NGOs, the Northern Region had consistently reduced HIV/AIDS prevalence, and now had the lowest prevalence rate (0.7%) in the country. On 28 July, former US president, Jimmy Carter, issued a press statement from the Carter Center in Atlanta to congratulate Ghana on stopping the transmission of Guinea worm. WHO would monitor this over a period of three years before declaring the country totally free of infection. In August, the government distributed 161 ambulances to district hospitals. As part of National Family Planning Week, on 28 September, DFID announced support for family planning measures that would benefit 690,000 Ghanaians over a year. Starting from October, the Ghana Health Service was to receive the first part of a delivery of 2.5 m doses of injectable contraceptives and 66,350 doses of implant contraceptives provided by UKaid. It was estimated this would avert 178,000 unintended pregnancies.

Agricultural developments continued. Among other things, on 4 April, the University of Ghana Research Centre at Okumening publicised findings on preserving fresh oranges for 60 days in the open. On 16 May, Japan donated 125 agricultural tractors with matching implements, ten rice mills, 35 rice threshing machines, 35 rice reapers, two combine harvesters and 40 irrigation pumps worth $ 5.1 m, under a scheme for grant assistance for underprivileged farmers. MOFA directed that the equipment be sold to farmers at reduced prices. On 11 August, the ministry of trade and industry announced that Ghana's banana exports had reached 65,000 tonnes per year. On 17 November, Ghana and IFAD signed a $ 31.5 m agreement to scale up the first and second phases of the Rural Enterprise Project.

The effects of *climate change* have regular environmental and economic impact. It was reported on 30 May that more than 6,000 buildings, including schools, were destroyed by rainstorms in the Upper East Region alone. On 11 July, a team of 75 US army personnel, including 20 doctors, began a ten-day joint medical outreach with colleagues from Ghana's 37 military hospitals and the National *Disaster Management* Organisation (NADMO). This operation took place under the Medical Field Logistics Assistance Group programme to promote interoperability between the two sides, and involved undertaking medical, dental and veterinary outreach services in three communities in Dangbe West, as well as classroom instruction, field training and mass casualty exercises. On 26 October, *floods* from torrential rain exposed the poor drainage system in Accra, leaving 14 people dead and 43,087 affected in other ways. NADMO responded on 31 October by distributing relief items to victims. It was estimated that the flood insurance claims amounted to $ 20 m.

Continual gestures were made to bridge the *north/south divide* through development. The Millennium Development Authority (MiDA) invested over $ 5.3 m in the Tamale Water Extension Project for the Tamale metropolis and other districts in MiDA's intervention zone in the Northern Region. On 30 March, the president launched a GHS 90 m rural electrification project for the Upper West Region at Siiriyiri. A similar project in the Northern Region also began a few weeks later, to support the plans of the Savannah Accelerated Development Authority to transform the area. On 13 May, the Ghana Airport Company announced that Tamale Airport would be upgraded into an international airport. The government announced on 18 June that 129 senior high school girls from the three northern regions were to benefit from a GHS 74,000 scholarship scheme to guard against drop-out. On 22 June, the Environmental Protection Agency announced in Tamale that the three northern regions were to benefit from a $ 15.23 m sustainable land and water management project to reduce land degradation and enhance biodiversity. On 13 April, the GNA reported that the US had provided $ 1.5 m for a 7.5 km road linking Wa East to Nadowli, involving the construction of a steel bridge and two concrete bridges, to be completed in seven months by PW Ghanem Construction.

On 12 April, Crown Prince Haakon and Crown Princess Mette-Mariti of Norway visited Accra, and announced a grant of $ 6.5 m to the Ministry of Environment, Science and Technology, to address environmental challenges in oil exploration. On 13 April, a $ 350,000 agreement was signed in Accra between the Bank of Ghana and the Swiss government, representing the latter's support for the development of a web-based collateral registry facilitating access to credit for *small and medium-sized enterprises* (SMEs). The agreement was part of $ 1.25 m support from the Swiss government to the IFC, which is implementing the Secured Transactions Project with the Bank of Ghana, to ease access to finance for SMEs. The facilitation follows on from Ghana's Borrowers and Lenders Act 773, which was passed in 2008 to establish the collateral registry currently hosted by the Bank of Ghana. On 10 August, a € 3 m agreement was signed in Accra for DANIDA to support the advocacy project for SMEs through the Business Sector Advocacy Challenge (BUSAC) Fund Phase II. DANIDA, which had already committed $ 8 m to the advocacy project, is the leading organisation under BUSAC II, together with USAID, which recently contributed $ 3 m as co-donor.

On 16 July, Ghana and France signed three financing agreements in Accra during French Prime Minister Francois Fillon's two-day official visit, to support various sectors of the Ghanaian economy. The agreements were for a loan of € 40 m, and a grant of € 500,000 for the Ghana Urban Management Pilot Programme. Agreements were also signed for the funding of two local banks: CAL Bank ($ 10 m) and Fidelity Bank Limited ($ 8 m).

Ghana was the second largest export market for *South African goods* in West Africa, after Nigeria. During President Mills's visit to South Africa on 23 August, the host officials stated that exports of goods and services from South Africa to Ghana had grown from about $ 138 m to $ 416 m in ten years.

On 20 October, Ghana and Turkey signed a $ 1 bn trade agreement to strengthen bilateral trade. The two countries set themselves three years to achieve targets set by the Ghana-Turkey Joint Economic Commission in trade, agriculture and tourism. Turkey would assist Ghana to build capacity and infrastructure in these and the petroleum sectors. This followed the first meeting of the joint commission in March, when President Gül of Turkey visited Ghana with a delegation of 108 officials.

On 23 October, during a four-day official visit by Cuban Vice President Estaban Lazo Hernandez, Ghana signed a memorandum of understanding with Cuba for the training of 250 Ghanaians as *medical doctors*. The medical students were to be selected from deprived districts, where they would be appointed on completion of training.

On 21 December, Ghana signed a pre-feasibility studies contract with Inekon Group of the Czech Republic to undertake a three-month comprehensive study on potential *tram routes*. The studies carried potential for awarding contracts for tram links in a number of Ghanaian cities.

Adverse reports about Chinese companies generated public concern. It was reported on 9 September that the Tesano Divisional Police were investigating Chinese staff at the Chinese furniture company Bedmate for almost killing a Ghanaian co-worker, and it was reported on 2 October that the China Jiang

International Construction Company, which was building a road at Akatsi, had been ordered to stop because the company was failing to comply with Ghana's *labour laws*. In December, the minister of lands and natural resources ordered a halt to developments that had encroached on the Ghana Atomic Energy Commission site, including one by the Chinese company Anainia, which had laid claim to a 164-acre plot at Dome-Kwabenya, where the nuclear facility is situated.

Mish Aviation Flying School, the first private *aviation* school in West Africa, was established in Tema Community 22 at the beginning of July to train senior high school graduates as full commercial pilots, using Cesna 172 aircraft. The institute would use the Federal Aviation Administration syllabus of the US Department of Transport. It was estimated that training would cost $ 58,652 per student for a maximum two-year training period.

Ghana in 2012

Kwesi Aning & Nancy Annan

The campaign for the 7 December presidential and parliamentary elections was the key event of the year. Although the elections were generally peaceful and both local and international election observers deemed the process to be free, fair and transparent, the campaign activities leading to polling day were marred by derogatory statements and speeches laced with ethnocentric epithets. This eventually led to several violent clashes between the two major political parties, the National Democratic Congress (NDC) and the New Patriotic Party (NPP). The sudden death of President John Evans Atta-Mills, however, contributed to a period of national unity, sorrow and calm, albeit short-lived. While election campaigns were the primary focus of activities, the country further consolidated its diplomatic and bilateral relations at subregional, regional and international levels.

Domestic Politics

The country's domestic politics were skewed towards preparations for the December elections and its related activities. On 24 March, the Electoral Commission (EC) began a biometric *registration exercise* as part of the preparations for the election. The three-month (March–May) registration exercise was fraught with challenges, although EC Chairman Dr Kwadwo Afari-Gyan continuously assured Ghanaians of an effective and well-organised registration. On 26 March, for example, there were reports of dysfunctional laptops, printers and fingerprint machines at some

 | DOI 10.1163/9789004308183_010

registration centres and, on 11 April, two leading members of the NPP, Ursula Owusu and Abu Jinapor, were attacked by hired party thugs, popularly known as 'machomen', at a registration centre in the Odododiodio constituency in Accra. On 22 June, the EC reported between 12,000 and 15,000 double registrations during the voters registration exercise and on 15 November, with a few weeks to go to the election, admitted that some minors, particularly in the Ashanti and Volta regions (strongholds of the NPP and NDC respectively), had been registered. Regardless of these challenges, the EC registered over 14 m potential voters and dedicated the period between 1 and 10 September to displaying the register for verification and correction.

In the interim, the *political climate* continued to be tense, marked by inter- and intra-party conflicts, political innuendo, violent clashes and the use of insulting and abusive language. On 19 January, President Mills fired Attorney-General and Minister of Justice Martin A.B.K. Amidu for accusing his administration of covering up "gargantuan economic crimes" against the state. On 11 June, Nana Konadu Agyemang Rawlings, wife of former president Jerry Rawlings and an NDC presidential aspirant who lost to Mills at the 2011 Sunyani Congress, announced the formation of her own political party, the National Democratic Party (NDP) and, on 12 October, she resigned from the NDC to take up the leadership of the NDP. This led to several objections from NDC supporters, who accused Rawlings, her husband and their followers of treachery.

Political break-ups and tensions did not only occur within the NDC. On 2 February, Paa Kwesi Nduom, former presidential candidate of the Convention People's Party (CPP), announced the formation of a new group, the Progressive People's Party (PPP), to contest the elections. This decision hinged on an internal power struggle within the CPP, which had escalated in the latter part of

2011, resulting in Nduom's eventual resignation. On 22 November, tensions within the People's National Convention (PNC) saw the denunciation of Hassan Ayariga, the party's presidential candidate, by some members of the leadership, including Atik Mohammed, the PNC's policy analyst. This denunciation came in the wake of allegations of Ayariga's close ties with the NDC and his misconduct at the second of three rounds of election debates at the Institute of Economic Affairs on 21 November.

Counter-attacks and clashes between loyalists of the ruling NDC and the opposition NPP escalated in the course of the year. On 19 January, Sunyani East constituency executives of the NPP reported attacks by supporters of the NDC. The NPP reported several attacks by NDC loyalists in the Odododiodio constituency, which occurred on 4, 12 and 19 March and led to numerous injuries. Similarly, there were reports of *violent clashes* between NDC and NPP loyalists at the Makola market and Kwame Nkrumah Circle in Accra on 11 and 13 December, respectively. The former incident resulted in the death of an NDC supporter. On 19 November, there were reported clashes between supporters of the NDC and NPP in the Efutu constituency in the Central Region.

Despite the intense political atmosphere, the year also marked the passing of two prominent statesmen. First, the announcement of the *death of President Atta-Mills* on 24 July threw the nation into a state of shock and mourning. While this period united many Ghanaians, there was indignation at the NDC's alleged deception over the president's health and the extreme pressures placed on him to run for re-election. The president's health status had been an open secret since the presidential elections in 2004, but many people were still dismayed by his sudden death. Atta-Mills was finally laid to rest on 10 August at the new 'Asomdwee' (Peace) Park near the Christiansborg Castle, Osu, in Accra. Second, on 16 November, the death was announced of former vice president John Aliu Mahama of the previous Kufuor-led administration.

In accordance with the provisions of the 1992 constitution, Vice President John Dramani Mahama was *sworn-in* as the interim president, less than 24 hours after the announcement of the president's death. Subsequently, on 30 August, President Mahama was unanimously elected as the new presidential candidate of the incumbent NDC, polling 99.5% of the votes at a special congress in Kumasi.

The selection of *presidential running mates* became an issue of central importance. In the NPP, there was speculation that the presidential candidate, Nana Akuffo-Addo, would change his running mate, Mahamudu Bawumia, for the 2012 election. There were reports of rival potential candidates for the NPP's vice presidential slot. These included former head of the Ghana Football Association, Alhaji MND Jawula; Deputy Minority Leader Ambrose Deri; and former Salaga MP Boniface Saddique Abubakar. On 29 March, Nana Akuffo-Addo formally retained Bawumia as his running mate, while Mahama announced on 18 September that Paa Kwesi Amissah Arthur Bekoe, a former governor of the Bank of Ghana and a native of the Central Region, would stand as his running mate, although Hannah Tetteh, a former minister of trade, was also seen as a potential candidate. On 12 September, 11 October and 17 October, the PPP, CPP and PNC selected three women, Eva Lokko, Sherita Sarpong and Helen Matrevi, as their respective vice presidential candidates. The CPP's selection of Sherita Sarpong, Queen Mother of the Dormaa Traditional Council, was in contravention of the 1992 constitution, which banned the active participation of chieftaincy office holders in politics. She subsequently resigned her queen mother position to compete in the elections.

Two *female presidential candidates*, Nana Konadu Agyemang Rawlings of the NDP, and Akua Donkor of the Ghana Freedom Party were, however, disqualified by the EC for not completing their registration forms. On 25 October, the former filed a case against the EC, which was, however, dismissed by the Human Rights High Court on 30 November.

With barely three months to the elections, Mahama began his campaign with the slogan, "Still a Better Ghana Agenda" and started by touring the Greater Accra Region on 19 September. Mahama's campaign tour to the Upper East Region from 10 to 12 November was perhaps the most controversial. On one of his campaign platforms in Zuarungu, the president was quoted as having asked the electorate to vote for him because he was a northerner. This sparked nation-wide condemnation. On 12–13 November, the PNC and NPP condemned Mahama's *ethnocentric politics*, and the CPP demanded an apology from the president on 15 November. To assure northerners of his support and discredit Mahama's ethnocentric outburst, Nana Akuffo Addo dispatched Bawumia, also a northerner, on a campaign tour in the three northern regions on 22 November. In his speech at one of his campaign stops in Walewale, Bawumia was reported to have remarked, "I ask you to vote for Nana and I, not because I am a northerner but because Nana and I have the vision, competence and incorruptibility necessary to solve your problems." Another NDC campaign controversy occurred on 12 November, when a renowned pastor, Mensa Otabil, condemned the party for wrongfully using his past sermons in its campaign commercials against Akuffo-Addo's free senior high school policy. This resulted in abusive comments from NDC officials, who called Mensa Otabil a "coward" and a "disappointment" and an ally of the NPP.

The *NPP campaign* was not without controversy, either. On 13 April, an "ethno-defamatory" and "treasonable" speech by Kennedy Agyapong, an NPP MP for Assin North, threatened the already fragile political atmosphere. In his speech, Agyapong was alleged to have said, "We would beat all Gas and Ewes in the Ashanti Region if this is how they want us to go. Again I declare war in this country (…). We would club any intruder who intends fomenting trouble with a machete and butcher them." As a consequence, civil society groups, religious bodies and political parties – especially the NDC – criticised the MP for "inciting war". He was arrested on 15 April and charged with genocide and treason. However, on 6 July, the case was rejected by the Supreme Court. On 1 August, Akuffo-Addo re-echoed his earlier "all-die-be-die" speech, made in 2011, defiantly defending the hostile mantra. The speech called on the party faithful to "take all necessary actions", including violence where needed, to defend themselves during the election. In addition, on 11 October, Akuffo-Addo visited ex-president Rawlings, founder of the NDC, which also sparked several debates. Critics perceived this visit as a desperate measure by the NPP to solicit the support of Rawlings and his followers.

On 4 September, the EC came under attack over the submission of constitutional instrument CI 78 to parliament. CI 78 authorised the EC to add 45 *new constituencies* to the existing 230, making a total of 275. Political parties doubted the legitimacy of this move and accused the president of using the constitutional process to rig the elections. Nevertheless, CI 78 became law on 2 October. On 14 October, the NPP organised primaries to elect candidates for the new constituencies, while the NDC had already organised its primaries on 5 August, i.e. well before CI 78 was passed. On 14 November, the *Electoral Commission* was censured for its delay in releasing the voters register. The Commission's tardiness fuelled doubts about its ability to organise a free and fair election, particularly when there were allegations of vote rigging by the government party. On 22 October, two EC directors were arrested for allegedly receiving bribes from a political party. On 29 November, the NPP alleged that workers of the National Disaster Management Organisation were transporting illegal ballot boxes, ballot papers and motorcycles to the northern region with the aim of preventing the EC from carrying the official ballot boxes to the polling centres.

Because of the tense atmosphere, civil society groups made a commitment to work for a peaceful election. On 15 February, the West Africa Network of Peacebuilding launched an 'Election Dispute Management Practice Guide for West Africa'. This guide was aimed at highlighting the causes and effects of election violence, as well as the mechanisms appropriate for resolving election-related disputes. On 18 July, the Institute for Democratic Governance organised a seminar on 'Ghana's Political and Administrative Transitions of Government'. Similarly, on 23 October the Kofi Annan International Peacekeeping Training Centre organised a colloquium on 'Ensuring Peaceful Elections in Ghana'. At the end of the colloquium, all stakeholders published a communiqué outlining their commitment to peace and calling on the government to use effective mechanisms to ensure a violence-free election. On 27 November, the National Peace Council, under the auspices of the Asantehene, Otumfuo Osei-Tutu II, organised a high-level meeting with all presidential candidates in Kumasi, urging them to take cooperative action against "electoral violence, impunity and injustice" and to abide by the results of the vote.

Of the 23 parties that campaigned at the beginning of the year, the EC only allowed eight to participate in the elections. With regard to the parliamentary elections, the EC announced on 3 December that 1,332 *candidates*, made up of 1,198 men and 134 women, had been approved. On 4 December, special voting commenced for security service and affiliated personnel who would be on duty on polling day. On election day, 4,000 non-partisan election observers were deployed by the Coalition of Domestic Election Observers, a civil society organisation, and over 20,000 police and 5,000 military personnel were also deployed by the government. External observers such as the AU deployed 40 observers, while ECOWAS and the West African Civil Society Forum (WACSOF) deployed over 250. Despite the use of biometric registration, voting was extended to 8 December owing to technical glitches.

As in 2008, the *parliamentary results* for the 2012 elections represented a setback for the NPP. Despite the electorate's tendency to go for a "skirt-and-blouse" vote, i.e. vote for the presidential candidate of one party and the parliamentary candidate of another, the NPP lost the parliamentary elections to the NDC. The NPP took 123 parliamentary seats to the NDC's 147, although this was an improvement for the NPP over the 107 seats it won in 2008. Samia Nkrumah, the only CPP MP in parliament and daughter of Kwame Nkrumah, lost her seat in the Jomoro constituency to the NDC's Francis Kabenlah Anaman. She blamed her loss on an invasion of the constituency by non-Jomoro residents on election day.

Mahama won the *presidential vote*. He received 50.7% of the votes, while the NPP's Akuffo-Addo received 47.7%. The PPP's Paa Kwesi Nduom took third place with 0.6% of the votes, while Henry Herbert Lartey, leader of the Great Consolidated Popular Party, came fourth with 0.4%. Before these results were announced by the EC, the NPP organised a press conference on 8 December declaring Nana Akuffo-Addo the winner, but the next day the EC officially declared John Mahama the winner of the 2012 elections. This result and declaration tallied with what observers and other tabulations had predicted, but the NPP protested that the results were not valid and was advised to file its complaints in court as provided for under the rules governing elections. Subsequently, on 28 December, the party filed its petition alleging electoral fraud with the Supreme Court.

Foreign Affairs

2012 was a busy year for the Mills-Mahama administration as far as diplomacy was concerned. The year began with invitations to attend *investiture* ceremonies in two West African countries. On 16 January, Mahama, on behalf of then President Mills, attended the inauguration ceremony of Ellen Johnson Sirleaf of Liberia. Mills himself attended the investiture of Macky Sall of Senegal on 3 April.

Ghana continued to show its commitment to the ideals of *ECOWAS* and the *AU*. The coups d'état that occurred in Mali and Guinea-Bissau in March and April, respectively, led to a series of ECOWAS meetings and consultations. On 27 March, Mills attended an extraordinary Summit of ECOWAS heads of state and government in Côte d'Ivoire to address the worsening crisis in Mali. Similarly, on 3 May, Mills attended an emergency summit of ECOWAS heads of state and government in Senegal to discuss the conflict situations in Mali and Guinea-Bissau. Mills also participated in the 18th ordinary session of the AU assembly of heads of state and government in Ethiopia (29–30 January). In his address, he emphasised the need for an increase in intra-Africa trade and effective mechanisms for improved inter-continental economic relations. Mills also unveiled a statue of Kwame Nkrumah in the forecourt of the AU headquarters.

Mills engaged in several *bilateral talks*. On 29 March, he embarked on a one-day working visit to Togo to hold talks with President Faure Gnassingbe. On 11 May, Mills received President Boni Yayi of Benin for talks on various issues. This meeting led to the signing of an agreement on energy supplies to Benin on 8 September by President Mahama. In addition, Ghana's long-standing bilateral relationship with South Africa was consolidated when the latter's Vice President Kgalema Motlanthe paid a courtesy call on Mills on 20 April to strengthen political and economic relations. The meeting ended with a promise from South Africa to support Ghana by providing 500 affordable housing units and to boost the country's tourism industry through the development of the Mole Game Reserve. At the global level, Mills was hosted by

US President Obama at the White House on 8 March for discussions on bilateral relations and regional integration. One of the key outcomes of the meeting was the signing of the Partnership for Growth Initiative, which was expected to increase and sustain mutual economic growth. Another outcome was the signing of a $ 1.2 bn facility with General Electric and the Conti Group for the energy sector. On 21 April, Mills once again travelled to the US as a Special Guest at the International Conservation Caucus Foundation forum on the promotion of good governance and natural resource management. Mills continued to New York on 26 April for a meeting with the Business Council for International Understanding. To further affirm their bilateral relations, Mills was invited by Obama to participate in the 38th G8 Summit at Camp David in May. On 1–3 March, a Chinese delegation held talks with Mills on strategies to strengthen bilateral relations and, on 13 December, Ghana signed a $ 30 m agreement with China for the construction of a 15,000 capacity stadium in Cape Coast.

From 22 to 28 September, newly sworn-in John Mahama was in the US to participate in the *United Nations* General Assembly meeting. During the six-day trip, Mahama held meetings with UN Secretary-General Ban Ki-moon, UNDP Administrator Helen Clark, World Bank President Jim Y. Kim and various heads of state, as well as business leaders. More importantly, on 26 September, Mahama addressed the 67th UN General Assembly. In his address, he recounted Ghana's progress towards the achievement of the MDGs, including poverty reduction, gender equality, access to safe drinking water, universal basic education and efforts to combat HIV/AIDS.

On 11 December, Mahama received President of Benin and Chairman of the AU Assembly Boni Yayi. The high-level delegation commended Mahama and the Ghanaian people for organising yet another successful election. On 12 December, Mahama travelled to Malabo (Equatorial Guinea) for the 7th Summit of the ACP heads of state and government. The meeting also marked the end of Ghana's four-year chairmanship of the ACP, which Mahama subsequently handed over to the government of Equatorial Guinea. At the meeting, Mahama urged world leaders to make an extra commitment towards peace and security, development and good governance. He also used the opportunity to encourage the ACP states to vote for Allan Kyeremanteng, a former NPP presidential aspirant, in the election for the executive directorship of the WTO. On 13 December, Mahama visited Abuja (Nigeria) for discussions with President Goodluck Jonathan on the West African Gas Pipeline.

Socioeconomic Developments

On 16 February, President Mills gave a state of the nation address on the theme "Still a Better Ghana Agenda" in which he highlighted his government's unprecedented economic achievements. He referred to the construction of 1,700 classroom blocks, distribution of over 60,000 laptops to schools, and a $ 7 bn growth in FDI. His statement on corruption was, however, received with uproar by the opposition, citing allegations of increasing amounts of *judgment debt* ordered to be paid by the government to aggrieved contractors, and lack of transparency. Since taking office in 2009, the Mills government had been accused of spending over GH¢ (cedi) 600 m Ghana on 'preventable' judgment debts, needlessly causing the state financial loss. The scandal surrounding these judgment debts escalated in 2012. On 16 January, Alfred Agbesi Woyome, allegedly a financer of the NDC, was accused of defrauding the state of some GH¢ 51.2 m. In addition, on 12 July, the former attorney general and minister of justice under the Mills/ Mahama administration, Betty Mould-Iddrisu, was accused of paying over € 94 m judgment debts to the Construction Pioneers company without due process and cabinet approval. The government blamed the increasing judgment debts on the previous NPP administration, which it accused of having illegally abrogated contracts.

Inflation remained stable in the first quarter, despite the 15% rise in petroleum prices in December 2011 and the 17.3% depreciation of the cedi. However on 9 May, Philomena Nyarko, acting government statistician, announced an inflation increase from 8.8% in March to 9.1% in April, indicating a rise in commodity prices. By November, inflation had risen again to 9.3%. The country experienced an *economic growth* rate of 7.1%, with the service sector showing the highest rate at 8.8% and the agricultural sector scoring the lowest at 2.6%. On 16 November, a report by the Ghana Monetary Policy Committee highlighted that, as of September 2012, the country had accrued revenues and grants totalling GH¢ 11.1 bn, and merchandise export growth of $ 10.1 bn, compared with $ 9.8 bn in 2011. Gold was the highest export commodity registering $ 4.1 bn.

Efforts were made towards improving *agricultural activity*. On 15 February, Mills opened the George Walker Bush Highway, part of a $ 547 m US Millennium Challenge Account (MCA) project to connect farming communities to commercial centres. The MCA project also supported the capacity building of farmers in 23 districts in the northern region. A $ 2.5 m Perishable Cargo Centre began operating on 16 February, aimed at providing storage for perishable foods, such as fruit and vegetables, for export. On 27 September, a critical access road, the Achimota-Ofankor road, was completed. On 29 October, the government reported a 30% reduction in rice imports and a corresponding 59% increase in local rice production.

The *oil and gas sector* brought in $ 340 m, compared with $ 347 m in 2011. On 14 December, the US-based Hess Petroleum company reported five new oil discoveries in the Deepwater Tano basin, Cape Three Points. The energy sector also received some external support. On 28 September, Ghana signed a $ 1.5 m grant agreement with South Korea for human resource capacity building to strengthen domestic energy transmission. In addition, on 14 November, Shell established a $ 2.2 m hydrocarbon storage facility at the Golden Star Resources, Bogoso Mines, and Air Liquide, an industrial and medical gas producer, opened a € 2 m liquid oxygen, nitrogen and argon plant and a 60 tonnes carbon dioxide storage tank at Tema on 3 December. On 5 December, a UK firm, Mere Power Nzema, announced an initiative to build a solar plant at Nzema. The $ 400 m facility was expected to increase power generation by 6%. Nevertheless, frequent power outages remained as the main challenge in the energy sector. As part of a national energy conservation mechanism, power rationing (also known as 'load shedding') was implemented during the greater part of the year, but this affected manufacturing output. The government blamed the power outages on the damage caused to the West African Gas Pipeline by an unidentified ship on 28 August.

Increasing *drug trafficking* received further international attention. On 18 May, Assistant US Secretary of State for International Narcotics and Law Enforcement William R. Brownfield travelled to Ghana to finalise discussions on the West Africa Cooperative Security Initiative. By 23 July, the US had begun training an anti-drugs police contingent in Ghana. Despite these efforts, £ 200,000 worth of cocaine was seized at Kotoka airport on 11 September and 7.5 kg of cocaine from Ghana was intercepted at Heathrow airport on 25 September.

On 12 November, Ghana signed a $ 12 m loan agreement with the Saudi Fund for Development to facilitate the construction of a trauma and acute care centre at the Korle-Bu Teaching Hospital. After acquiring a 70% share in Ghana Telecom, the main challenge of Vodafone UK was the increasing incidence of cable theft. On 26 November, the management announced that over 34 'mega cables' containing about 2,500 smaller cables had been stolen in August alone. Frequent cable theft cost the company over GH¢ 2 m annually. On the positive side in telecommunications, on 23 November, Minister of Communications Haruna Iddrisu unveiled ten mobile communication towers provided by K-NET to service rural communities.

Ghana in 2013

Kwesi Aning & Nancy Annan

The principal political issue in 2013 was the challenge brought by the New Patriotic Party (NPP) against the Electoral Commission (EC) in the Supreme Court and the way this impacted on the country's democracy and security. Economic growth was affected by rising inflation, which resulted in popular dissatisfaction with President Mahama's economic policies. Throughout the year, the government of the ruling National Democratic Congress (NDC) was confronted with allegations of corruption, including the infamous "Victoria Hammah saga"; a leaked recording of a telephone conversation revealed that a deputy minister of the ruling party was hoping to receive $ 1 m before leaving office. The country continued to consolidate its bilateral ties and abide by its bilateral and multilateral obligations, both in Africa and across the world.

Domestic Politics

An *electoral petition* filed by the NPP against the EC at the Supreme Court on 28 December 2012 took centre stage in many of the country's political debates during 2013. In the petition, the NPP, led by its presidential candidate, Nana Addo Danquah Akuffo-Addo, alleged that irregularities had been found in 24,000 electoral results sheets (known as the pink sheets), which skewed the outcome in favour of the NDC. On 3 January, the NDC was joined in the court action as the matter also involved them.

Despite the inevitable political tensions, the Office of the Chief Justice, in accordance with the provisions of the 1992 Constitution,

 | DOI 10.1163/9789004308183_011

proceeded with preparations for the *investiture* of President John Dramani Mahama and he was sworn in on 7 January. The ceremony was attended by numerous foreign dignitaries, former president and NPP leader John Agyekum Kufuor, and representatives of various political parties. However, the NPP decided to boycott the ceremony, labelling it an "illegal swearing in". On 9 January, NPP members said Kufuor's attendance had betrayed the party.

Immediately after his inauguration, Mahama began the process of selecting his cabinet. In accordance with Article 78 of the Constitution, Mahama submitted his first batch of ministerial nominees to parliament on 12 January. By 14 February, a total of 28 ministers had been appointed, which rose to 85 ministers and deputy ministers by 28 March. As a result, Mahama was accused of breaking his promise to run a lean government and of appointing numerous people of questionable competence. Assibey Yeboah, MP for New Juaben South, remarked on 28 March: "The *size of government* is just too big . . . almost every major Ministry has two Deputies; Finance, Lands and Forestry, Agriculture . . . just jobs for the boys." He further accused the president of vacillating throughout the selection process. A political scientist at the University of Ghana argued that the cabinet should not number more than 40 ministers. However, the Constitution's silence on the issue made it difficult to control appointments.

On 16 April, Mahama marked his *first 100 days* in office. Political parties, think tanks, civil society organisations and the media differed on his achievements. On 15 and 18 April, NGOs such as the policy thinktank IMANI and the Ghana Centre for Democratic Development gave the president approval rates of 47% and 67% respectively. However, on 20 April, the editor-in-chief of the 'New Crusading Guide' wrote: "There is nothing to write home about in the 100 days, and it is even in the interest of government that we don't do an assessment." Members of the NDC and other parties were also against an assessment, arguing that an evaluation after 100 days in office, a practice that had begun during the Kufuor presidency in 2001, represented an *unfair benchmark*. Thus, on 18 April, members of the People's National Convention questioned the fairness of the practice.

While the president marked his 100 days in office, the Supreme Court commenced the hearing of the NPP's *election petition* against the EC (16 April). The case attracted a lot of attention, as it was believed that the ruling would reflect the degree of Ghana's democratic maturity. To ensure transparency, the hearing was broadcast throughout the country from the day it began until the pronouncement of the verdict. Interestingly, the petition hearing revealed inefficiencies and bottlenecks in the electoral system. The petitioners accused the EC of several discrepancies, including duplication of serial numbers in 8,987 out of the 10,119 polling stations, lack of biometric verification during voting, and absence of signatures of the EC's presiding officers on some of the pink sheets. Some of these allegations were admitted by the EC. The admission on 4 June by Afari Gyan, the EC chair, of 50 cases of double registration in records of 705 Ghanaians in the diaspora was a case in point. Perhaps the advantage of such revelations was the fact that they could serve as lessons learnt for future elections. The non-partisanship, unbiased attitude and professionalism demonstrated in the *Court hearing* also proved a formative experience. Thus, on 2 July, the president of the panel of judges, Justice William A. Atuguba, sentenced Ken Kuranchie a journalist and alleged NPP supporter, and Stephen Atugiba, member of the NDC, to ten- and three-day jail terms, respectively, for contempt of court. This ruling to some extent transformed citizens' perception of the Court and reinforced their trust in the judiciary, which prior to the case had been widely seen as corrupt and unfair.

The *Court's verdict*, eight months after the closely contested election, constituted a test for the country's democracy. Political tension increased as the date of the verdict drew near. Civil society organisations, traditional rulers, the clergy, government and security officials and political parties all campaigned for peace to be maintained. On 23 August, the Ghana Police Service deployed 32,000 personnel across the country to curb any violent clashes and prevent the eruption of potential conflict. On 29 August, the Supreme Court issued a verdict in favour of the EC and NDC. The Court indicated that the petitioners had not shown adequate evidence to substantiate their case and argued that the inaccuracies in the electoral system were not sufficient to "discredit" the final results. Nana Addo Danquah Akuffo-Addo demonstrated political maturity by gracefully accepting defeat, despite disagreeing with the Court's ruling. The demonstration of national loyalty by the various stakeholders during the judicial process confirmed Ghana's political development, potentially further consolidating the democratic system. While the Supreme Court ruling led to celebrations in the NDC camp, it sparked an *intra-party backlash* within the NPP. Members blamed each other for the 2012 election defeat and the failure of the subsequent court case. Noting the simmering tensions within the party, Nana Addo Danquah Akuffo-Addo and his vice-presidential candidate, Mahamudu Bawumia, implored party loyalists during their country-wide 'Thank You Tour' on 14–22 September to "never speak ill of any fellow party member as that would only lead to cracks in the party". Nevertheless, party members and the leadership continued to trade accusations. On 24 September, the former NPP MP for Mfantseman West, Stephen Asamoah Boateng, criticised his party's general secretary, Kwadwo Owusu Afriyie, for causing divisions in the party and for mocking him for his defeat in the 2012 elections. Subsequently, on 25 September, the NPP national chairman, Jake Obetsebi Lamptey, in a letter to the party entitled 'An Open Letter to the NPP Members and Supporters: New Patriotic Party, Thoughts on the Way Forward', accused party followers of being their "own worst enemies". In addition, on 2 October, an NPP youth faction called Patriotic Future of NPP launched an attack on the party's executives, accusing them of thievery and calling them "self-seeking individuals" who caused the party's defeat. Nana Addo Danquah Akuffo-Addo's candidature as the party's standard-bearer for the 2016 election also became a dividing factor. Members who did not support Akuffo-Addo's candidature felt sidelined and pressured to accept him. On 16 October, Stephen Asamoah Boateng alleged that some party leaders were cajoling him and other members into accepting Nana Akuffo Addo as the 2016 presidential candidate.

The *NDC* was also *hit by feuds*. On 30 April, a conflict between NDC members in the Sissala East Constituency of the Upper West Region, which had begun in 2009, resurfaced. Clashes between the former NDC MP, Rafatu Alhassan Dubie, and his successor, Alijata Sulemana Gbentie (who was then also the district chief executive), escalated, with the latter setting up her own executives, so that the party's executive body in the region was divided into two. On 4 September, loyalists of late president John Atta-Mills expressed their discontent by reportedly accusing Mahama of "destroying the party", and plotting to challenge his 2016 candidature.

Corruption allegations levelled against the NDC by the general public and the opposition over its misappropriation of state funds increased party discontent. For example, on 1 November, verbal clashes within the NDC reached a crescendo when long-standing party member and MP for Nadowli-Kaleo Constituency in the Upper West Region, Alban Bagbin, accused the president of not dealing effectively with corruption and not making himself accessible for advice on the issue. This led to a violent backlash from other members of the party, who called Bagbin a "liar" and an "enemy within". These clashes abated when the party's general secretary, Johnson Asiedu Nketia, called for a truce on

5 November and established a committee to investigate Bagbin's claim.

Against this background, it is significant that NPP-NDC clashes were few. Despite its internal controversies, the NPP began preparations for the 2016 general elections by conducting countrywide *party elections* for its polling station, constituency and regional executives. Elections for polling station and constituency executives were held from 1 to 30 November and 14 November to 28 December, respectively. Regional and national executive elections were scheduled for early 2014. Generally, the elections were conducted peacefully and smoothly, with the exception of some constituencies in the Volta and Northern regions where polls had to be rescheduled due to misunderstandings and voting irregularities.

Foreign Affairs

On 19 September President Mahama took part in the investiture of Ibrahim Boubacar Keïta as Mali's newly-elected president. He also attended the 21st AU summit in Addis Ababa (Ethiopia) on 24 May, which also commemorated the 50th anniversary of the establishment of the (O)AU. On 17–18 July, he attended the 43rd ECOWAS summit in Abuja (Nigeria). Ghana's commitments to *UN peacekeeping operations* received new recognition when on 14 June 700 Ghanaian peacekeepers were awarded medals by Special Representative of the UN Secretary-General Karin Landgren for their exceptional services to the UN Mission in Liberia since the beginning of the mission in 2003.

The Mahama administration intensified its bilateral engagements. On 6 May, Ghana and *Japan* signed a $ 14 m funding agreement for the advancement of the Power Distribution System project in Brong Ahafo and the three Northern regions. This was followed by the president's participation, with the First Lady Lordina Mahama, in the 5th Tokyo International Conference on African Development in Yokohama (1–3 June). During the conference, Lordina Mahama attended, with other First Ladies, the International Symposium on HIV and AIDS. On 21 June, Ghana and the *US* signed a $ 1.4 m project agreement towards the advancement of research in agriculture and agribusiness. US Secretary of State John Kerry and Mahama had a bilateral discussion on 26 September at Kerry's official residence in New York on the progress of the Millennium Challenge Account (MCA) and future American energy support to Ghana. This meeting followed the signing of an $ 8 m Memorandum of Understanding between Ghana and the Millennium Challenge Corporation on 23 July with a view to undertaking feasibility studies for the second compact of the US-funded MCA.

The president also engaged in *sub-regional collaboration*, particularly with regard to maritime piracy and energy. On 9 August, Mahama attended a meeting of heads of state and government in Malabo (Equatorial Guinea) concerning maritime security along the Gulf of Guinea. The meeting was convened by President Teodoro Obiang Nguema Mbasogo of Equatorial Guinea in the wake of rising piracy activities along the Gulf. Participating countries discussed collaborative efforts to strengthen security in their territorial waters and curb piracy. In view of the energy deficit affecting most African countries, states along the Gulf of Guinea organised the 16th Gulf of Guinea Gas Conference in Abidjan (Côte d'Ivoire) on 6–8 November. The president was represented by Minister of Energy and Petroleum Emmanuel Armah-Kofi Buah, who encouraged delegates to pool their energy resources. The meeting also called for exchange of knowledge and experience and the formulating of strategies regarding gas production for industrial development.

On 20 September, Mahama departed for the 68th Session of the *UN General Assembly* in New York, which ran from 23 September to 3 October. It took place under the theme 'Post-2015 Development Agenda: Setting the Stage'. Mahama addressed the Assembly, calling on the international community to understand the uniqueness of African culture and values with regard to democracy. The Assembly was also attended by former president Kufuor. During the same trip, Mahama attended the 60th anniversary celebration on 25 September of the Africa-America Institute, an institution dedicated to promoting education and professional training for many African countries including Ghana. Furthermore, the president used his visit to the US to deliver a lecture on 'Ghana's Evolution as a Democracy and its Growing Economic and International Influence' at Kennesaw State University, Atlanta, Georgia, on 1 October, as part of efforts to establish more academic relationships with foreign educational institutions.

Relations with *South Africa* were strengthened. On 5 November, Mahama dispatched Minister for Foreign Affairs Madam Hannah Tetteh to the 3rd South Africa-Ghana Permanent Joint Commission for Cooperation meeting in Pretoria. The meeting resulted in bilateral talks between Hannah Tetteh and South Africa's Minister of International Relations and Cooperation Maite Nkoana-Mashabane on on-going partnerships and future collaboration. The Permanent Joint Commission meeting was followed by a three-day state visit to Ghana by President Jacob Zuma on 25–27 November to strengthen the bilateral relationship. South Africa is the 14th largest investor in Ghana with investments between 2003 and 2013 totalling some 64 m South African rand. The main highlight of the visit was the signing of a Memorandum of Understanding on 26 November, affirming cooperation in air services, transport, electricity and energy.

The death of former South African president *Nelson Mandela*, on 5 December 2013 marked a sad end to the year. Ghana mourned the death of this iconic leader. In an interview with the 'New York Times' on 6 December, Mahama expressed his sorrow over Mandela's death, recognising his great leadership on Africa's journey towards democracy and good governance. He reportedly remarked: "His utilisation of peace as a vehicle of liberation showed Africa that if we were to move beyond the divisiveness caused by colonisation, and the pain of our self-inflicted wounds, compassion and forgiveness must play a role in governance."

Mahama concluded the year's diplomatic engagements by attending the Elysée summit on peace and security in Paris (France) on 6–7 December, an initiative of President François Hollande to consolidate Franco-African relations, especially with regard to their joint commitment to peace and security. In his speech, Mahama called for collective efforts to address security on the continent as development cannot be achieved in "an environment of maritime piracy, terrorism, rebel activities, drug and human trafficking". Almost 40 African leaders attended the two-day summit.

Socioeconomic Developments

On 21 February, Mahama delivered his state of the nation address and, like his predecessor, promised to tackle corruption across all sectors of the economy, stating "our commitment to the fight against corruption remains unshakeable". Despite these promises, corruption within state institutions increased. On 16 July, an investigative report was submitted by a five-member ministerial committee set up on 12 April by Minister of Youth and Sports Elvis Afriyie-Ankrah to assess allegations of *financial mal-*

practices at the Ghana Youth Employment and Entrepreneurial Agency (GYEEDA), known under the Kufuor administration as the National Youth Employment Programme. It proved the first of many tests of Mahama's anti-corruption campaign. The report, which was initially alleged to have been suppressed until it was leaked to the public, accused two NDC cronies, Abuga Pele, former GYEEDA national coordinator, and Clement Kofi Humado, MP, of involvement in a multi-million dollar scheme affecting the administration of the agency. They were said to have made payments of over $ 2 m to local companies whose work could not be accounted for. The report also revealed that several officials and companies working for the government were engaged in "bribery, corruption and circumvention of due processes". It added that the government was paying these companies over 1,200% interest a year without regard to national bidding procedures. The report also disclosed that interest-free loans of Ghana cedi (GH¢) 50 m (over $ 19 m) had been given by the Mahama government to Roland Agambire, a close ally of the president and CEO of RLG (a computer assembling company that served as one of GYEEDA's service providers). While many people expected the president to demonstrate leadership by prosecuting the offenders, they were disappointed when on 30 July Mahama announced the formation of another committee to review the initial findings. On 20 December the deputy attorney general indicated that RLG would be sued if it did not refund the loan within a year.

On 28 October, the private radio station 'Joy News', after nine months of investigation, exposed corrupt practices in one of Ghana's leading public hospitals, Korle-Bu. Its broadcast accused hospital officials of taking "*bribes from patients* to reduce their bills significantly and divert the money into their private pockets". Such protracted corrupt practices had for decades impeded the effective services provision to the general public.

Another corruption scandal that hit the headlines was a leaked telephone conversation that took place on 7 November, in which Mahama's Deputy Minister of Communications Victoria Hammah indicated that she had been granted her position on a silver platter as a result of her contacts in the NDC's inner circles. She also revealed her aspiration to use her position to make at least $ 1 m before leaving office. After the tape's release, the president was accused of selecting incompetent officials and dealing ineffectively with corruption within his government. On 8 November, Hammah was relieved of her duties.

GDP did not reach the expected 8% growth but stopped at 6.7% in the first quarter of 2013 (compared with 10.3% in the same period of 2012). By June, GDP had fallen to 6.4% before ending the year at 7.4%, according to Price Waterhouse Coopers' report on Ghana's 2014 Budget. The service sector reported a higher growth rate (12%), followed by 1.1% in agriculture and a reduced *growth* rate of 0.8% in industry. According to the Ghana Statistical Services third quarter report, production of oil, gold and diamonds plummeted by 16.0%, 29.7% and 2.9%, respectively. The 2014 budget published by the Ministry of Finance and Economic Planning on 19 November highlighted the steady rise in *inflation* from 10.1% in January to 13.1% in October. Another worrying trend, which was to be underscored by the president's 2014 state of the nation address, was the excess in commodities *imports*. Mahama noted that the country spent "almost $ 1.5 bn in foreign currency on importing rice, sugar, wheat, tomato products, frozen fish, poultry and vegetable cooking oils. Rice accounted for $ 374 m, fish $ 283.3 m, wheat $ 226.7 m, poultry $ 169.2 m, cooking oils $ 127 m, and tomato products $ 112.1 m."

As a result, public concern over the government's economic management ability increased. The ruling party quickly responded to public disaffection by blaming the reduced economic growth on the election petition case. On 7 September, for example,

Deputy Minister of Information and Media Relations Ibrahim Murtala Mohammed stated that productivity had declined over the period of the petition case because many citizens were watching the live broadcast. He also indicated that the live screening of the hearing cost the Ghana Broadcasting Corporation over GH¢ 3.5 m ($ 1,341,900), which had affected the state's finances. In fact, however, the fall in economic growth was the result of a combination of factors, including inflation and the fall in value of the cedi.

On 27 November, the Bank of Ghana Monetary Policy Committee report indicated that *revenue* and grants for the year totalled GH¢ 13.9 bn ($ 5.3 bn). No breakdown of revenues per sector and commodity was provided.

With the country's increasing *agricultural and energy* challenges, the government intensified initiatives to improve these two sectors. On 3 January, it inaugurated an 80-tonnes capacity warehouse for food storage in Bazua, a community in the Upper East region, funded by the Alliance for Green Revolution in Africa as part of the Ghana Arzakinmu Programme, to provide training and storage facilities for communities in the Volta, Northern, Upper East and Upper West regions. The programme had so far led to the construction of warehouses in 18 communities and the training of 12,327 small-scale farmers across the four regions. Similarly, on 19 December, the president inaugurated the multi-million dollar Bui Hydro Power Project, which was anticipated to produce 400 MW of power to help resolve chronic energy problems. The project, which began in 2008, was funded with a concessionary loan ($ 263.5 m) from China and buyer's credit ($ 298.5 m) from EXIM Bank, with an additional contribution of $ 60 m by the government. The dam would also make possible the irrigation of 30,000 ha of farm land.

In December, the National Disaster Management Organization reported that there had been 478 incidents of fire across the country, affecting 11,766 people, most of whom were market women. It also recorded floods, which displaced over 6,000 people in 44 communities in the northern part of the country.

The government increased initiatives to fight *drug trafficking*. On 31 January, the former UN Secretary-General, Kofi Annan, launched the West Africa Commission on Drugs in Accra. Despite these efforts, there were reports of large amounts of cocaine being shipped into the country. On 19 November, a ship from Guyana was seized, which was reportedly carrying 414 kg of cocaine, worth over $ 50 m worth.

Illegal artisanal mining by foreigners, especially Chinese immigrants, led to violent clashes with locals: on 9 May, two Ghanaians were killed by Chinese miners over a contested plot of land in Obuasi, Ashanti Region. On 14 May, President Mahama established an inter-ministerial taskforce to address the issue, and on 20 June the government arrested and deported 269 foreigners (218 Chinese and 51 Nigerians). At year's end the number of *Chinese deportees* had risen to 4,500.

Printed in the United States
By Bookmasters